MENTORING FOR RESILIENCY

SETTING UP PROGRAMS FOR MOVING YOUTH FROM "STRESSED TO SUCCESS"

Nan Henderson,
Bonnie Benard,
Nancy Sharp-Light
Editors

Foreword by Emmy Werner

Published by
Resiliency In Action, Inc.

Preface

by Nan Henderson, M.S.W.

During a presentation a few years ago in Dayton, Ohio a school board member asked me, "If resiliency is so real, why are our young people struggling so?"

This book provides a research-based, in-depth answer to that question. More importantly, it provides information about how families, schools, agencies, churches, and all youth-serving organizations can turn the situation around.

I answered the board member this way: "Young people need certain things in their lives to foster their resiliency. I have diagramed these in The Resiliency Wheel. For many young people, the strands of The Wheel, which represent resiliency builders as well as basic human needs, are to a large degree, missing. What needs to be done is this: Put each young person in the center of The Wheel, and begin weaving as many strands as possible in as many places as possible in his or her life."

I developed The Wheel (Figure 1) as a visual representation of what numerous studies show people need to successfully meet life's challenges, including bouncing back from the stresses along the way. Even though our world has "progressed" in many ways during the past decades, we have paid a price. The strands of many people's Resiliency Wheels have been strained by the fast-paced, highly transitory, individual-achievement focus of our present culture.

Young people feel this loss most acutely. In short, many of them are not experiencing the strands of The Wheel, which show up in these or similar terms in almost all of the discussions by youth experts about what is necessary for "positive youth development."

The most important strand of The Wheel—the foundation upon which the

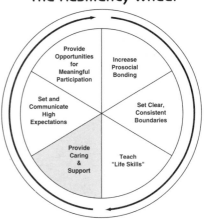

Figure 1:
The Resiliency Wheel

Adapted from the book, Resiliency in Schools: Making It Happen for Students and Educators *by Nan Henderson and Mike Milstein, published by Corwin Press, Thousand Oaks, CA (1996)*

other strands are built—is *caring and supportive relationships*. When I ask resilient young people, some of whom speak out in this book, about how they bounced back from drug use, violence, school failure, and teen pregnancy, they always first name *the people who made a difference for them*. They talk with animation about the qualities of these people, about how they not only expressed consistent, non-judgmental caring, but also how they empowered, inspired, and provided a mirror and model of what could be.

A crucial message in this book is that the quality of person-to-person relationships is the most important consideration in fostering youth resiliency. A concern expressed throughout is that it is not enough just to provide "resiliency-building," "asset-promoting" structures (programs) for kids. Our work must go deeper.

As Bonnie Benard so eloquently puts it in her chapter on "How to Be a Turnaround Teacher/Mentor":

> Resilience research points out over and over that transformational power exists not in programmatic approaches per se, but at the deeper level of relationships, beliefs and expectations, and the willingness to share power. In other words, it is how adults do what they do that counts.

It is our hope that this book will add this crucial focus to the current national effort to provide more "youth programs." The programs described herein are examples of approaches that work. To some degree their success can be attributed to an effective structure. But more importantly, these programs succeed because at their core are caring, supportive, empowering relationships—the single most important factor in moving youth from "stressed to success."

Nan Henderson, M.S.W.
San Diego, CA
March, 2000

Foreword

by Emmy Werner, Ph.D.

Research on resilient children and youth has repeatedly shown that if a parent is incapacitated or unavailable, other significant people can play an enabling role in a youngster's life, whether they are grandparents, older siblings, stable child care providers, competent and responsible peers, teachers, elder mentors, or youth workers. In many communities, it may make better sense to strengthen such informal ties to kith and kin than to introduce additional layers of bureaucracy into the delivery of services, and it might be less costly as well.

Programs that Promote Resiliency

Research has also shown us that the promotion of resiliency in children by caring adults does not rely on aiming to remove stress and adversity completely from their lives, but rather in helping them enlarge their repertoire of problem-solving and social skills, which, in turn, will enhance a youngster's sense of self-efficacy and self-esteem. Programs that pursue these objectives seem to work best in the context of an organized and predictable environment that combines warmth and caring with a clearly defined structure and the setting of explicit (time) limits.

> *"In many communities, it may make better sense to strengthen such informal ties to kith and kin than to introduce additional layers of bureaucracy into the delivery of services, and it might be less costly as well."*

Project Head Start, the largest nation-wide early intervention program established for children of poverty, even today, serves only one out of three of those who are eligible for the program. In high quality programs it fosters many of the protective factors that have brought about positive changes in the lives of "at risk" children.

A promising example of a Head Start-based "peer treatment" program has been reported by researchers from the University of Pennsylvania (Fantuzzo, Coolahan, & Weiss, in press). They paired maltreated and socially withdrawn preschool children with more socially adept and responsive peers in Head Start programs that were supervised by parent assistants. The investigators demonstrated a significant and lasting increase in social interactions and a decrease in solitary play for these children under the influence of their more outgoing peers.

Several national evaluation studies have also documented positive effects on both "at risk" youngsters and foster grandparents who are participants in the **Domestic Volunteer Service** which works mostly with hospitalized and abused children and in daycare programs for homeless and immigrant children. Infants with foster grandparents were easily comforted and became strongly attached to their foster grandmothers; toddlers showed improvement in motor and social development; preschool children made gains in cognitive development and social competence. For the foster grandparents, in turn, the experience with the children in their care was associated with improved life satisfaction, health, and vigor (Werner, 1997). Similar positive results have been reported for school-age children who are being tutored by older adults who work as members of the **Experience Corps** in inner city schools around the country (Freedman, personal communication).

> *"Competence, confidence, and caring can flourish, even under adverse circumstances if youngsters encounter caring persons who provide them with the secure basis for the development of trust, autonomy, initiative, and above all, hope."*

As explained in chapters one through four of this book, the positive effects of one-to-one mentoring on the lives of 10 to 16-year-old "at risk" youngsters has also been demonstrated in a nation-wide evaluation study of the **Big Brothers/Big Sisters** by Public/ Private Ventures, a Philadelphia-based policy research organization.

Another promising example, the California-based **Sister Friend Program**, is presently being evaluated. It matches teenage mothers with young women who voluntarily contribute of their time to link both mothers and infants with available community services. Tentative results suggest that the program makes a significant impact on the high school graduation rate and work status of the mothers and on the developmental status of their young children (Tebb, 1998).

Attributes of Successful Prevention Programs

Some 10 years ago, in her book *Within Our Reach*, Lisbeth Schorr identified seven attributes that are shared by programs that have successfully prevented poor developmental outcomes in children and youth who grew up in "high risk" families and communities: (1) They are comprehensive, flexible, responsive, and persevering; (2) they see children in the context of their families; (3) they deal with families as parts of neighborhoods and communities; (4) they have a long-term preventative orientation, a clear mission, and continue to evolve over time; (5) they are well managed by competent and committed individuals with clearly identifiable skills; (6) their staffs are trained and supported to provide high-quality responsive services; and (7) they operate in settings that encourage practitioners to build strong relationships based on mutual trust and respect.

In planning mentoring or any youth program, program planners may want to apply some of these criteria to the task of "resiliency building." We certainly know on the individual level from the life stories of the resilient youth we have studied that competence, confidence, and caring *can* flourish, even under adverse circumstances, if youngsters encounter caring persons who provide them with the secure basis for the development of trust, autonomy, initiative, and above all, hope.

But there is now a need to gather evidence that programs specifically designed to "foster resiliency" can actually affect lasting positive changes in the behavior of youngsters who grew up under the shadows of alcoholism, child and drug abuse, parental mental illness, family discord, chronic poverty, or disability. Shared catharsis among program leaders and program participants may be a good first step, but then they need to ask what specific behaviors or

> *"The move from exhortation to evaluation will provide us with the necessary evidence for building better programs and it will keep us humble, for there is no one magic bullet that transforms a vulnerable individual into a resilient one."*

conditions they want to change in the individuals who participate in their "resiliency-building" ventures.

The Move from Exhortation to Evaluation

After that they need to document, over time, whether these changes are taking place, whether these changes last, and what individual differences arise in the responses of the participants to their well-intentioned enterprise. The move from exhortation to evaluation will provide the necessary evidence for building better programs and it will keep those of us involved humble, for there is no one magic bullet that transforms a vulnerable individual into a resilient one.

> *"Forget about getting results overnight (or within an hour!). Take a longer view!"*

In this country there is a wealth of experience and knowledge that can be shared by clinicians who deal with specific individuals who overcome the odds and by professionals who want to improve the well-being of communities. They need to learn from each other about the design of the best programs possible and they need to share the evaluation of their effects (and occasional missteps) with policy makers who determine legislation on behalf of children and families. In that process, they may well need two more pieces of advice given by Lisbeth Schorr in her latest (1997) book *Common Purpose*: (1) The time has come to give up searching for a single intervention that will be the one-time fix, the life-time inoculation against adversity; and (2) Forget about getting results overnight (or within an hour!). Take a longer view! Just like the research on resiliency, program building and evaluation take time and perseverance, but also an attitude of hopefulness. ➤

References

Barr, R.G., Boyce T., & Zeltzer, L.K. (1994). The stress-illness association in children: A perspective from the biobehavioral interface. In R.J. Haggerty, L.R. Sherrod, N. Garmezy, & M. Rutter (Eds.), *Stress, risk, and resilience in children and adolescents* (pp. 182-224) New York: Cambridge University Press.

Fantuzzo, J., Coolahan, K.C., & Weiss, A.D. (in press). Resiliency Partnership directed intervention: Enhancing the social competence of preschool victims of physical abuse by developing peer resources and community strength. In D. Cichetti & S.L. Toth (Eds.), *The effects of trauma on the developmental process.* Rochester, N.Y.: University of Rochester Press.

Freedman, M. (1993). *The kindness of strangers.* San Francisco; Jossey-Bass.

Schorr, L.B. (1988). *Within our reach: Breaking the cycle of disadvantage.* New York: Anchor Books.

Schorr, L.B. (1997). *Common purposes: Strengthening families and neighborhoods to rebuild America.* New York: Anchor Books.

Tebb, K. (1998). One-on-one mentoring: A comparative study of outcomes for adolescent mothers and their children participating in Sister Friend and Cal Learn. Unpublished Ph.D. Dissertation in Human Development, University of California, Davis.

Tierney, J.P., Grossman, J.B., & Resch, N.L. (1995). *Making a difference: An impact study of Big Brothers/Big Sisters.* Philadelphia, PA: Public/Private Ventures.

Werner, E.E. (1997). The value of applied research for Head Start: A cross-cultural and longitudinal perspective. *National Head Start Association Journal of Research and Evaluation,1* (1).

Werner, E.E. (1999). Protective factors and resilience. In S. Meisels & J.P. Shonkoff (Eds.),*Handbook of Early Intervention* (2nd ed.). New York: Cambridge University Press.

Werner, E.E., & Johnson, J.L. (in press). Can we apply resilience? In M.D. Glantz, J. Johnson, & L. Huffman (Eds.), *Resilience and Development: Positive Life adaptations.* New York: Plenum Press.

Werner, E.E., & Smith, R.S. (1992). *Overcoming the Odds: High risk children from birth to adulthood.* Ithaca, N.Y: Cornell University Press.

Werner, E.E., & Smith, R.S. (1988). *Vulnerable but invincible: A longitudinal study of resilient children and youth.* New York: Adams, Bannister, Cox.

Werner, E.E., Randolph, S.M., & Masten, A.S. (1966, March). Fostering resiliency in kids: Overcoming adversity. *Proceedings of a Congressional Breakfast Seminar.* Washington, D.C: Consortium of Social Sciences Associates.

Emmy E. Werner, Ph.D., is a research psychologist at the University of California, Davis, and known as "the mother of resiliency" for her decades of work as a resiliency researcher. She is best known for her longitudinal study (with Ruth Smith) of all the children born on the island of Kauai in 1955, which still continues 45 years later. She has authored numerous publications, including those referenced above.

CONTENTS

Mentoring: New Study Shows the Power of Relationship to Make a Difference

by Bonnie Benard, M.S.W.

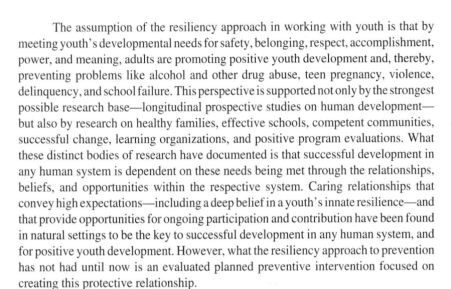

The assumption of the resiliency approach in working with youth is that by meeting youth's developmental needs for safety, belonging, respect, accomplishment, power, and meaning, adults are promoting positive youth development and, thereby, preventing problems like alcohol and other drug abuse, teen pregnancy, violence, delinquency, and school failure. This perspective is supported not only by the strongest possible research base—longitudinal prospective studies on human development—but also by research on healthy families, effective schools, competent communities, successful change, learning organizations, and positive program evaluations. What these distinct bodies of research have documented is that successful development in any human system is dependent on these needs being met through the relationships, beliefs, and opportunities within the respective system. Caring relationships that convey high expectations—including a deep belief in a youth's innate resilience—and that provide opportunities for ongoing participation and contribution have been found in natural settings to be the key to successful development in any human system, and for positive youth development. However, what the resiliency approach to prevention has not had until now is an evaluated planned preventive intervention focused on creating this protective relationship.

Public/Private Ventures (P/PV), a national not-for-profit research corporation based in Philadelphia, has published the fourth and final volume of its three-year, $2 million evaluation of Big Brothers/ Big Sisters of America (BB/BS)—an impact study of the oldest and most carefully structured mentoring effort in the U.S. According to the authors of the study, titled *Making A Difference*, "Our research presents clear and encouraging evidence that caring relationships between adults

> *"The most notable results are the deterrent effect on initiation of drug and alcohol use, and the overall positive effects on academic performance that the mentoring experience produced."*

and youth can be created and supported by programs, and can yield a wide range of tangible benefits" (p. iv). Furthermore, "The most notable results are the deterrent effect on initiation of drug and alcohol use, and the overall positive effects on academic performance that the mentoring experience produced" (p. iv). In essence, the resiliency/ youth development approach to healthy development and successful learning are validated in this scientifically reliable impact evaluation.

Study Overview

Briefly, P/PV, using a classical experimental research methodology with random assignment, conducted a comparative study of 959 10- to 16-year-olds who applied to BB/BS programs in eight geographically diverse cities in 1992 and 1993. Half of these youth were randomly assigned to a treatment group for which BB/BS matches were made or attempted; the other half were assigned to waiting lists. After 18 months the two groups were compared. Participants in a BB/BS program were less likely to start using drugs and alcohol; 46% less likely to start using illegal drugs; 27% less likely to start drinking. However, the effect was even stronger for minority Little Brothers and Sisters who were 70% less likely to initiate drug use than other similar minority youth! Little Brothers and Sisters were about one third less likely than controls to hit someone. They skipped half as many days of school as did control youth, felt more competent about doing schoolwork, skipped fewer classes, and showed "modest gains in their grade point averages"—with the strongest gains among minority Little Sisters (p. iii). Lastly, they improved their relationships with both their parents and their peers relative to their control counterparts.

Of particular note is that probably all of these youth—both treatment and control groups—would be considered "high risk" youth:

- 90% lived with only one of their parents;
- over 80% came from impoverished homes;
- over 40% received either food stamps and/or cash public assistance;
- 40% came from homes with a history of alcohol and drug abuse;
- nearly 30% came from families with a record of domestic violence; and
- nearly 30% were victims of emotional, physical, or sexual abuse.

Conversely, the Big Brothers/Big Sisters were generally well-educated young professionals. About 60% were college graduates; nearly two thirds had a total household income over $25,000 (with 40% over $40,000). Also of note, about three fourths of the volunteers were white. In essence, despite this enormous social distance between the youth and the volunteers, they were able to establish successful relationships—across their class and race differences. To what, then, does P/PV credit this accomplishment?

The three earlier studies in P/PV's four-part evaluation of BB/BS answer this question. These earlier studies looked respectively at (1) program practices (implementation of the program model), (2) volunteer recruitment and screening, and (3) the

> *"Sustained relationships were those in which the mentor saw him/herself as a friend, not as a teacher or preacher."*

nature of the relationships between volunteers and youth (how they form, are sustained, and end). From these earlier examinations the researchers attribute the successful outcomes to two overall characteristics: the one-to-one relationship and the program's supportive infrastructure.

Characteristics of Effective One-to-One Relationships

First of all, the relationship was of sufficient *intensity*. From my 15 years of reviewing prevention evaluation research, the lack of intensity is continually identified as a barrier to positive results. However, in the 400 matches studied here, more than 70% of the matches met three times a month for an average of 3-4 hours per meeting and 50% met one time a week. This comes to around 144 hours of direct contact a year, not counting telephone interaction.

Secondly, even though this outcome study did not examine the nature of the relationship between the adult and youth, the third companion study (*Building Relationships With Youth in Program Settings*, May, 1995) illuminated the nature of the relationships that were of sufficient intensity and duration to produce these effects. Certainly coming as no surprise, but presenting powerful validation of the resiliency perspective, is the finding of this third study that sustained relationships were those in which the mentor saw him/herself as a friend, not as a teacher or preacher (IV, p. 51). These "developmental" relationships were grounded in the mentor's belief that he or she was there to meet the developmental needs of youth—to provide supports and opportunities the youth did not currently have.

> While most developmental volunteers ultimately hoped to help their youth improve in school and be more responsible, they centered their involvement and expectations on developing a reliable, trusting relationship, and expanded the scope of their efforts only as the relationship strengthened (III, p.ii).

These volunteers placed top priority on having the relationship enjoyable and fun to both partners. Furthermore, they were "there" for the young person, listened nonjudgmentally, looked for the youth's interests and strengths, and incorporated the youth into the decision-making process (gave them "voice and choice") around their activities. From a resiliency perspective, they provided the three protective factors of a *caring relationship* that conveys *positive expectations and respect*, and that provides *ongoing opportunities for participation and contribution*—and saw risks existing in the *environment*, not in the youth.

In contrast to these developmental relationships (fortunately, two thirds of the 82 relationships examined were developmental!), were the "prescriptive" relationships in which the adult volunteers

> **"Serving the needs of mentors is as important as serving the needs of youth."**

believed their primary purpose was guiding the youth toward the values, attitudes, and behaviors *the adult* deemed positive. "Adults in these relationships set the goals, the pace, and/or the ground rules for the relationship. These volunteers were reluctant to adjust their expectations of the youth or their expectation of how quickly the youth's behavior could change" (III, p. iii). A majority of these prescriptive volunteers were basically there to *fix kids*—typically to improve school performance—and most of their shared time was spent in conversation—not fun activities—around grades and classroom behavior. For these volunteers, risk lay within the youth:

What seemed to stand out for these prescriptive volunteers was less the deficiencies present in the youth's environment, and more, particularly in terms of morals and values, those present in the youth themselves—deficiencies prescriptive volunteers frequently sought to rectify (III, p. 40).

Not surprisingly, the adults and youths in these matches found the relationship frustrating and nonsupportive. Of these prescriptive relationships, only 29% met consistently (compared to 93% of the developmental) and at the 18-month follow-up, only 32% were ongoing (compared to 91% of the developmental) (III, p. 18). What is particularly frightening in reading some of the interviews with the youth and the prescriptive volunteers is the fact that these relationships are probably doing more harm than good—are becoming themselves another risk factor in an already stressed young life as illustrated by the following poignant statements:

Youth: When I went out with my Big Brother he... said okay, let's go get the library card and let's go to the library and check out a book. But I stayed at the library all day and he kept coming back, and telling me I didn't have the right information. So I studied there until closing time in the library. I was sitting there doing a report on toads and frogs, and when he came back, I had my report done, but I didn't have a rough draft. So like I wrote word for word out of the book; he said that's cheatin'.

Interviewer: He said that's cheating?

Youth: I just sat there and dropped in tears.

Interviewer: You started crying?

Youth: I mean it's something that I just can't hold them in...

Interviewer: What upset you about that?

Youth: I don't know. I didn't wanna stay there, I felt like I was supposed to write the report in my own words. Like some of it I got out of the book and some of it came out of my own head... I had to do it over.

Interviewer: You had to do it over?

Youth: Yeah, and he picked me up from the library and it was raining. (III, p. 63)

In contrast, this is the voice of a developmental volunteer:

[When he told me about a bad grade] I kind of focused on his other grades first; he said that he had done a good job with the other ones. And then I asked him if he wanted to do better in it, and then I kind of asked him how he could do better. And it was a pretty simple thing because he just didn't do a couple reports. So we decided that, you know, the next ones he got I would help him with them if he wanted. And we did that twice. You know, so it's like what can we do together to do this... When I came home with even a B or even an A-, sometimes it would be well, why did you get a minus here. It wasn't like, oh you did great. So I was sensitive to that (III, p. 59).

The youth-centered approach—asking the youth what he needed and wanted— and then offering help as a shared activity, as well as the strengths-focus, sensitivity, and empathy displayed by this volunteer stands in sharp contrast to the earlier volunteer who didn't ask what the youth wanted, who left the youth alone and on his own with no assistance, who clearly had decided the youth should spend time at the library, and who displayed only insensitivity and lack of empathy. According to the researchers,

> That participation in BB/BS was able to achieve transformative goals [outcomes like reduced alcohol use] while taking a general developmental approach lends strong support to the emerging consensus that [ironically!] youth programs are most effective in achieving their goals when they take a more supportive, holistic approach to youth" (III, p. 51).

Certainly, this study proves the deep truth of Nel Noddings' (1988) statement: "It is obvious that children will work harder and do things—even odd things like adding fractions—for people they love and trust" (p.32).

Program Infrastructure: "Prerequisites for an Effective Mentoring Program"

From the studies of BB/BS' program practices and recruitment and screening as well as earlier Public/Private Ventures' research on mentoring, the researchers conclude that "the following program irreducibles are prerequisites for an effective mentoring program":

- Thorough volunteer *screening* that weeds out adults who are unlikely to keep their time commitment or might pose a safety risk to the youth
- Mentor training that includes *communication and limit-setting* skills, tips on *relationship-building,* and *recommendations on the best way to interact with a young person*
- Matching procedures that take into account the preferences of the youth, their family, and the volunteer, and that use a professional case manager to analyze which volunteer would work best with which youth
- *intensive supervision and support of each match by a case manager* who has frequent contact with the parent/guardian, volunteer and youth, and provides assistance when requested or as difficulties arise (IV, p. 52)

Supervision is a hallmark of the BB/BS approach to mentoring... [and] "the program practice most associated with positive match outcomes" (I, p. 61). The earlier study found that those sites following the BB/BS procedures for regular supervision had matches that met at the highest rates; those agencies that reduced this function had problems. As several studies of mentoring have discovered, serving the needs of mentors is as important as serving the needs of youth; you can't have one without the other! According to Ron Ferguson's (1990) study,

> Most programs expect to use volunteer mentors to supplement the love and attention that their paid staffs provide to children, but those that have tried have experienced only limited success at finding mentors and keeping them active. *They have discovered that fulfilling mentors' needs is as important for sustaining their involvement as fulfilling youths' needs is to sustaining theirs* (p. 15).

This is a finding directly paralleling what educational researchers have found about meeting the needs of teachers as a fundamental prerequisite to engaging students!

Another critical benefit of having paid staff is the stability and continuity they provide. Case managers ensure that youth are not left on their own if their mentor leaves. In fact, several investigators have found that even in programs that employ volunteer mentors, it is the case managers/youth workers that are often the real mentors to youth (Freedman, 1993; Higgins et al., 1991; Ferguson, 1990).

Implications for Prevention, Education, and Youth Development

 The youth development/resiliency approach is key to successful learning and social development.

Perhaps the finding with the greatest implication for prevention and education is the power of a *non*-problem-focused intervention to produce positive—and superior—results compared to the targeted problem-focused interventions that dominate the prevention field, from substance abuse to dropout, to teen pregnancy, to violence prevention.

> Participation in a BB/BS program reduced illegal drug and alcohol use, began to improve academic performance, behavior and attitudes, and improved peer and family relationships. Yet the BB/BS approach does not target those aspects of life, nor directly address them. It simply provides a caring, adult friend. Thus, the findings in this report speak to the effectiveness of an approach to youth policy that is very different from the problem-oriented approach that is prevalent in youth programming. This more developmental approach does not target specific problems, but rather interacts flexibly with youth in a supportive manner (IV, p. 1).

I would extend this conclusion to the whole youth-serving arena, including families and schools. The development of a caring, trusting, respectful, reciprocal relationship is the key to reducing risks, enhancing protection, and promoting positive youth development in *any* system.

 Creating "mentor-rich" environments must be a major focus.

As I stated in an earlier work on mentoring, an approach to mentoring especially compelling to me is the concept of infusing mentoring—as a way of being with youth—into social institutions: families, schools, and communities. This would create what Marc Freedman (1993) [see chapter two] refers to as "mentor-rich environments"—environments that create lots of opportunities for young people to interact with an array of caring adults must be the focus.

> *"The development of a caring, trusting, respectful, reciprocal relationship is the key to reducing risks, enhancing protection, and promoting positive youth development in any system."*

> Creating mentor-rich settings—schools, social programs, youth organizations—is one way of moving beyond the chimera of super-mentoring, in which a single charismatic adult is called on to be a dramatic influence, providing all the young person's needs in one relationship. In reality, young people need more than one relationship to develop into healthy adults (p. 111).

He states,

> Our aspiration should be to create planned environments conducive to the kind of informal interaction that leads to mentoring. Indeed, such an approach is rooted in the historic strength and traditional practice of extended and fictive kin structures in many low-income communities—particularly African-American neighborhoods (p. 112).

What this means is expansion of the world of adult contacts for all youth in their natural environments. This means supporting families in their efforts to parent via family-centered social policies that promote flexible work policies, parental leave, time off to work in schools, decent wages, family healthcare benefits, and quality child care. Communities must also create opportunities for youth to be directly involved with more adults through community service, work apprenticeships, more involvement in local government, and so on. Young people need more opportunities to interact and form relationships with the older generation—the generation that currently is abdicating its responsibilities to the young.

③ *Creating mentor-rich environments means relationships must be the central focus of reform efforts.*

Creating mentor-rich environments in schools, community-based organizations, and communities as a whole means relationships must be the top priority in any prevention effort or educational reform. As this study so eloquently proves, a focus on outcomes alone inevitably leads to youth-fixing, control strategies in our institutions—and often deleterious ones. For example, an outcome of reduced alcohol and drug use often leads schools to zero tolerance strategies which expel youth from school and push them onto the streets. At its extreme, this prescriptive approach leads to the imprisoning of more and more young people.

> *"[To] expand the world of adult contacts for all youth in their natural environments... means supporting families in their efforts to parent via family-centered social policies that promote flexible work policies, parental leave, time off to work in schools, decent wages, family healthcare benefits, and quality childcare."*

The BB/BS study, along with all the research on resiliency and positive youth development, shows clearly the path for youth policy and educational reform. Unless there is a focus on the mediating variables of relationships, beliefs, and opportunities for participation, the desired outcomes of reduced alcohol and other drug abuse, school success, and compassionate and responsible citizens will never be achieved. This is the key message of resiliency research and the BB/BS evaluation; this is the message to sell to preventionists, educators, youth and educational policy makers, and adult society. All these constituencies must see that (1) what works is known!, (2) it's never too late to transform young lives, (3) caring is not a "touchy-feely" add-on luxury but a critical necessity to educational and social change and perhaps the most important, and (4) adult society has a civic and moral responsibility to the next generation—to "other people's children."

Other People's Children

The last point remains the ultimate challenge. While mentoring programs, as the BB/BS evaluation shows, have demonstrated their power to promote healthy development and prevent problem behaviors, they ultimately serve only a few of the millions of children who could

> *"Relationships must be the top priority in any prevention effort or educational reform."*

benefit and have a hefty price tag of $1,000 a match. Moreover, they are a limited intervention in the realm of systemic social change. Just as disadvantaged children have been and continue to be socially created by policies that systematically deny them opportunities to succeed in society, to change this situation requires new social policies. These policies must address the most powerful risk factor a growing number of children and youth, and their families, face: poverty. Many policy experts agree with Stanley Eitzen's (1992) vision of just what these changes must look like:

> Since the problems of today's young people are largely structural, solving them requires structural changes. The government [and the government is all of us!] must create jobs and supply job training... as well as exert more control over the private sector. In particular, corporations must pay decent wages and provide adequate benefits to their employees.... There must be an adequate system for delivering health care, rather than our current system that rations care according to ability to pay. There must be massive expenditures on education to equalize opportunities from state to state and from community to community. There must be equity in pay scales for women. And finally, there must be an unwavering commitment to eradicating institutional sexism and racism (p. 590).

"What [mentoring] offers besides a transformational experience to the young people involved, is the opportunity to reconnect the young and old, to reweave the intergenerational threads that are essential to a healthy society."

That these systemic changes will be costly there is no disputing; however, far more costly will be society's refusal to pay what it costs to provide the developmental opportunities and supports all young people need. As Mike Males (1996) states in *The Scapegoat Generation*, his compelling investigation of America's War on Adolescence, "The deterioration in public support for families with children [is] a direct result of declining tax revenue and school funding [and] reverberates across generations" (p. 285). He claims, "America's level of adult selfishness is found in no other Western country," citing a 1995 National Science Foundation-funded study that found the U.S. ranking first in per-person affluence, "producing a higher gross domestic product with 250 million people than the other 17 nations, population 400 million, combined!" Furthermore, "The U.S., by an even larger margin, also ranks first in child poverty" (p. 7).

While mentoring is a limited intervention, Males acknowledges that "the path to intergenerational cooperation [is] difficult at this advanced state of deterioration..., it lies in *inviting* adolescents into adult society." Furthermore,

> What is needed is not a revolution of fiscal policy or remedial plan, but one of fundamental attitude. Nothing good will happen until elder America gazes down from our hillside and condominium perch and identifies the young—darker in shade as a rule; feisty; lustful as we were; violent, as we raised them to be; no different from us in any major respect—as our children" (pp. 291-292).

According to Freedman (1996), mentoring offers just this opportunity to identify and realize our shared humanity.

> Mentoring amounts to the "elementary school of caring" for other people's children, the children of the poor. It is a specific context in which to initiate the process of reconstructing empathy.... Mentoring brings us together—across generation, class, and often race—in a manner that forces us to acknowledge our interdependence, to appreciate, in Martin Luther King, Jr.'s words, that "we are caught in an inescapable network of mutuality, tied to a single garmet of destiny" (pp. 134, 141). ➤

References

Note: The Big Brother/Big Sisters evaluation was published in four volumes available through Public/Private Ventures, 2005 Market Street, Suite 900, Philadelphia, PA 19103; 215/557-4400:

I.   *Big Brothers/Big Sisters: A study of program practices* (1993,Winter).
II.   *Big Brothers/Big Sisters: A study of volunteer recruitment and screening* (1994, Fall).
III. *Building relationships with youth in program settings* (1995, May).
IV. *Making a difference: An impact study of Big Brothers/Big Sisters* (1995, November).

•••

Benard, Bonnie (1992). *Mentoring programs for urban youth: Handle with care.* San Francisco, CA: WestEd. (June).

Eitzen, D. Stanley (1988). Problem students: The sociocultural roots. *Phi Delta Kappan,* December, 296-298.

Ferguson, Ronald (1990). *The case for community-based programs that inform and motivate black male youth.* Washington, DC: The Urban Institute.

Freedman, Marc (1993). *The kindness of strangers: Adult mentors, urban youth, and the new voluntarism.* San Francisco, CA: Jossey-Bass.

Higgins, Catherine, et al. (1991). *I have a dream in Washington, D.C.: Initial report,* Winter. Philadelphia, PA: Public/Private Ventures.

Males, Mike (1996). *The scapegoat generation: America's war on adolescents.* Monroe, ME: Common Courage Press.

Noddings, Nel (1988). Schools face crisis in caring. *Education Week,* December 7, 32.

Bonnie Benard, M.S.W., has authored numerous articles and papers on resiliency. She can be reached at Resiliency Associates, 1238 Josephine, Berkeley, CA 94703, (p/f 510-528-4344), or by e-mail: bbenard@flashnet.com.

Mentoring as the Most Promising Prevention: An Interview with Marc Freedman

by Bonnie Benard, M.S.W.

In 1992 when I was researching the topic of mentoring, [see the related report on the Big Brothers/Big Sisters evaluation in chapter one], I discovered a Public/ Private Ventures' document by Marc Freedman, The Kindness of Strangers: Reflections on the Mentoring Movement *(1991). It was far and away the most comprehensive, insightful, and critical look at mentoring that had been written. In 1993 the document was expanded into the book,* The Kindness of Strangers: Adult Mentors, Urban Youth, and the New Voluntarism *(Jossey-Bass) which still remains the seminal work in the field. Freedman's understanding of the promise mentoring holds to create the caring relationships "between young and old" that Emmy Werner states are the key to effective prevention as well as the limitations of one intervention to rebuild the sense of belonging and community youth—and adults—are hungry for makes him, and his work, a valuable ally in spreading the resiliency message.*

BB: Marc, you played a seminal role in getting the Big Brothers/Big Sisters evaluation which validates the power of relationship to promote positive youth development, to happen. What got you personally interested in the concept of mentoring?

MF: It came through two different sources. One was doing research on youth service projects around the country. These urban youth service corps were organized in teams and each team had an adult supervisor or team leader. When I went out and did field work on those projects—especially interviewing young people—I was struck by how prominent the relationships with the team leader were in prescribing what they were getting out of the corps. It wasn't a one-on-one relationship, but it just seemed that in this program the critical ingredient for the young person's success was this relationship. I was struck at the same time by how rarely this *affective* aspect of programs is discussed in the program evaluation literature. I think [this is] primarily because evaluators of programs—and part of the reason for program evaluation—tend to come from economics and quantitative sociology. It has been very difficult to figure out how you could take account of those relationships.

So what I wanted to do with the book in part was to put what I was seeing in these programs [the importance of relationships] into the broader context and understand what kind of importance it could hold. It was really to try to bridge this gap between what young people were saying was important to them in the program and what was showing up on these evaluations which tended to focus much more on more impersonal aspects—especially the curricula.

BB: I think this is still the major challenge. I've been in the substance abuse prevention field, where they've spent lots of money on program evaluations—and they never look at relationships, only program content. I just read an *Education Week* article yesterday that was discussing the rise in illicit drug use of 12-17-year-olds and when they get around to discussing what to do, it's the same old list of curricula and canned programs. And then there's a book like your book and a study like this BB/BS evaluation as well as the many qualitative studies capturing the voices of youth—and they tell what is important.

MF: Right. In fact within the context of those drug reports, we know that beginning in 1992, drug use increased by 105%. And the two major responses seem to be that Dole has argued that what we need to do is greatly increase the military in the war on drugs and, basically, to get out the troops and batten down the border. And the Clinton response has been, as Barry McCaffree has been talking about, how we need a new propaganda push—more subway posters and celebrities telling them to say no. While I'm sure the Clinton approach is sounder, neither one of them take into account that *the only real way to reach teenagers is through real people*. They need to hear the message from adults. They don't need slogans from politicians or supposed role models or from the media. They need real relationships. I guess the greatest argument on behalf of that approach would be the Big Brothers/Big Sisters study because that occurred at exactly the same period that this drug use increased. It started in 1992, and we found by looking at a control group of kids who were on the waiting list with kids assigned Big Brothers and Big Sisters, there was a 40% decrease in those young people with Big Brothers and Big Sisters in starting to use drugs. And 40 % were from families that had a history of substance abuse; all were from single parent families; and they were predominately minority— African American—kids.

> *"The only real way to reach teenagers is through real people. They need to hear the message from adults. They don't need slogans from politicians or supposed role models or from the media."*

BB: All the ones labeled "high risk."

MF: Exactly. At the exact same period when drug use is doubling, we find that by providing consistent adult relationship, you get the exact opposite trend: Drug use is essentially cut in half as opposed to doubling. What's so striking about that is that we found in a separate in-depth study of relationships within the context of Big Brothers and Big Sisters, that the mentors who were most successful were not the ones who tried to promote the drug avoidance curriculum or tried to basically tell young people what to do, but the ones who just concentrated on becoming friends with the young people.

BB: This P/PV companion study on relationship is so powerful and totally validates all of the beliefs that I've been trying to put out there along with a bunch of other people, certainly starting with Emmy Werner—that *how* you are with the person makes the difference; that you need to develop that caring relationship and play to the strengths of young people and find their gift and give them opportunities to be involved and contribute and be reciprocal.

Now this is a question I have: Is it going to be difficult, given that the outcome study in Volume IV didn't look at the nature of relationships, to tease this very critical connection out? If that last outcome study could say, "OK. This is the *type* of relationship that gives us these really positive outcomes." It's that one little connecting piece that I want!

MF: I agree with you—it would be ideal if we had that kind of information in the last study because now it's really looking at the confluence of the different studies and trying to draw some conclusions.

BB: Frankly, it scares me that since this study is obviously already beginning to have impacts on federal and state policy (I think the California Department of Alcohol and Drug Programs is initiating something, as well as the Governor!)—people will go for the *program*, and they won't look at *how* the program is done as an important part. When I read those voices of the kids in the study on relationship, it scared me that some of those very prescriptive mentors—their attitudes in the way they work with the kids—would actually harm the youth! And the kids were so loving and still accepting of somebody that was really giving them negative messages.

MF: Absolutely. I think that there are three lessons we need to emphasize from this study. One is that the sustained kind of relationships that Big Brothers/ Big Sisters produces can have some real effect. Two is that you can only produce these relationships if you have programs that provide adequate screening and follow-up support. It takes a lot to produce a sustained relationship, and it costs a lot too. It costs about $1,000 a match. But we know from looking at Big Brothers/Big Sisters along with other kinds of mentoring that there is a dramatic difference in terms of the kind of care and attention that goes into a program like Big Brothers/Big Sisters. And the difference is that Big Brothers/ Big Sisters produces a lot more substantial relationships, a lot more frequent relationships. Three, you can produce these relationships only if you have mentors who focus

> *"At the exact same period when drug use is doubling, we find that by providing consistent adult relationship, you get the exact opposite trend: Drug use is essentially cut in half as opposed to doubling."*

on building a real relationship and not try to storm in and prescribe to young people how they should lead their lives.

BB: Do you see as a result of this evaluation that Big Brothers/Big Sisters will put more emphasis on screening and training people about relationship development?

MF: I think Big Brothers/Big Sisters has always emphasized that, and I think they'll get more money to do that—to screen and support more relationships than they were beforehand. Now they can go to funders with stronger evidence that the extra care they take is worth it. One of the reasons they were interested in having this study done is that a lot of other less careful mentoring programs are going to the same funders and claiming to be able to produce results with a lot less staffing.

But on the other side, there were some other lessons that came out of our research which suggests change within Big Brother/Big Sisters. A number of applicants who never make it to the Big Brothers/Sisters matching—about three quarters of the people who approach the program with an interest in helping young people—one way or another are either discouraged or weeded out before they get to being matched. In part, that is good. But in a lot of cases people get discouraged because it's so long from the time you apply until the time you're matched; a lot of people out there who probably would be good Big Brothers or Big Sisters are being discouraged. While a lot of these people might not be appropriate as a Big Brother/Big Sister, they could help kids in other ways.

> *"You can produce these relationships only if you have mentors who focus on building a real relationship and not try to storm in and prescribe to young people how they should lead their lives."*

BB: That's a lot of people who have the interest to even approach an organization like Big Brothers/Big Sisters. There are so many things that come out of your work that parallel Jeremy Rifkin's conclusions in his book, *The End of Work*. He states that in spite of the U.S. having perhaps the worst public policy support for children and families, the U.S. has the highest rate of voluntarism in the industrialized world. And something you pointed out in your book, the importance of mentoring as a way to get middle-class people—the ones that are isolating themselves in the suburbs—in touch with especially poorer young people and in some way build a movement—through voluntarism—that would support public policy changes around children and family issues.

MF: I agree with that although I have several responses. One of the striking discoveries for me in interviewing mentors is the extent to which mentoring can be a *social program for adults* under the guise of being one for kids. You suggested that maybe the adults who come forward to mentor, even though they're sympathetic to kids to start, have no idea what these young people are facing. In many cases, they end up learning as much as the young people, and in some cases they can become advocates on behalf of kids. The theme of Big Brothers/Big Sisters' conference this year was advocacy for positive youth development. They're trying to move more aggressively into having that potential within their movement. Part of what these mentors can do is work directly with kids, but in concert they might be able to help the wider community understand why it's important to fund better schools and youth programs and more youth programs.

On the other hand, there are some limits as to what volunteers can do. Voluntarism, even though it's a big part of American life, is declining. The last Gallop poll of 1993 showed over five years a decline of 54-48% in terms of the percentage of Americans who were volunteering. There was a decline in the number of hours that they're putting in and a decline of about 10 million volunteers during that period. I think that the main reason we're seeing that is just that people are working so hard.

BB: Exactly. That brings up Juliet Shor's book, *The Over-Worked American*, which relates directly to this issue.

MF: Shor's book says the average American works 164 more hours a year since 1971. That's almost an extra month a year. One of the ways that has impacted communities is that it's particularly women who are hard hit by the increase in working hours because the tremendous movement of women into the work force has reduced the amount of time available for women to volunteer. And for the last 100 years, women have been the mainstay of the volunteering movement. For example, PTA memberships have dropped from 12 million to 7 million over the last 30 years. As Arlie Hochild's work at UC Berkeley has shown, since women still continue to do most of the child rearing and domestic duties besides working outside the home, the average working woman works fifteen hours a week more than the man. Over a year that's an extra month of 24-hour days.

You can see why it's a lot harder to also add on that extra shift of being a Big Brother or Big Sister. So I think what Big Brothers/Big Sisters and the other mentoring programs try to do is to concentrate more on younger people before they've had kids and before they've gotten married. They have a lot of mentors in their 20s and early 30s and a lot of college students. The untapped resource, I think, is older adults, which you talked about earlier. At the same time there is a decrease in volunteer time for people in the middle generation, you have people retiring earlier, living longer, and remaining healthier who could make a huge difference in communities.

BB: And who are at a point in their lives—the stage of generativity—where they decide they've made their living and are looking for meaning and maybe what they can do to give back.

MF: Exactly. We lack the institution to engage that segment of the population. Partly our institutions have ignored the potential there. In groups like Big Brothers and Big Sisters, there are very few older adults. But then our culture has also degraded the idea of generativity; we have replaced it with the leisure village of recreation.

BB: And I don't know if children are even allowed in many of them! That seems to get to be a very scary dilemma, where you have so many older adults isolated from children and young people. I just read a new book by Mike Males called *The Scapegoat Generation: America's War on Adolescents*. He shows how most of the policies, and you can certainly see it in Clinton too, start blaming kids for problems like substance abuse, violence, etc.—that we blame them for their natural response to this society that we adults have created.

> *"Mentoring can be a social program for adults under the guise of being one for kids."*

He concludes from his carefully documented research that unless we can engage older adults to care for the next generation, our country is going to continue to decline in all indicators of health and especially in the sense of community belonging. For example, if you look at Florida, which I don't think any Democrat has won since Jimmy Carter, there's a state filled with retirees—many of whom are even afraid of young people. The walls have been erected so well. And he said that our ultimate challenge is to make the connection—to "rebuild the village."

You started to talk about Big Brothers/Big Sisters maybe moving more into an advocacy position. Do you know if the Federal Government is interested in this study and would be interested in putting more money into this in any way?

MF: There's tremendous interest within the Clinton Administration to try to support mentoring programs, and there was money in the Clinton Crime bill. There was money in the original welfare reform proposals that all would have gone for mentoring and relating these activities, and that was cut out by the Republican Congress. But through National Service there's enormous mentoring going on in a variety of different ways. Americorps has funded programs like Friends of the Children in Portland, Oregon, where Americorps serves as full time mentors for young people in the second grade and they actually spend time in the classroom with them. They provide a bridge between home, and they'll work with between four and eight kids.

There is also interest on the part of the National Service Corporation and Harris Walford, the president, in trying to use Americorps volunteers to help groups like Big Brothers/Big Sisters doing mentoring to recruit and screen and increase the number of those mentors who can be placed and supported. So that's a great opportunity there. In addition, the Corporation runs Foster Grandparents. There are 25,000 foster grandparents that work one-on-one each year with 90,000 kids, making them actually bigger than Big Brothers/Big Sisters. In fact, it's the biggest one-on-one program for kids in the country. It's also a program that Emmy Werner is a huge fan of, and I am as well.

> *"The untapped resource...is older adults....At the same time there is a decrease in volunteer time for people in the middle generation, you have people retiring earlier, living longer, and remaining healthier who could make a huge difference in communities."*

It's a program for low-income older adults, almost entirely women over the age of sixty-five. And since its beginning as a War on Poverty program, it's mandated that the foster grandparent volunteers have to work one-on-one with disadvantaged or disabled young people.

But you know on the bipartisan side, there are a number of Republicans who are really interested in mentoring as well. To give you an idea of the national bipartison appeal, two Senators who are former Big Brothers are Christopher Dodd on the one hand, who is one of the leading liberals in the Senate, and Dan Coates from Indiana, who is one of the most high-profile conservatives. In fact, Coates has proposed a bill which would pour substantial amounts of Federal dollars into Big Brothers. So there is some potential bipartisan interest.

BB: You know in some way the whole idea of relationships and what mentoring stands for is so deeply human that no matter who you are or your political values, it strikes at your heart and your deep sense of what it is to be a human being and what's important in life. Any of us alive and any of us functioning know that we have to thank our relationships for being here. However, you coined the term "the over-selling of mentoring"—that mentoring can divert attention from needed policy reforms that would address restructuring our youth-serving institutions.

MF: The great fear I have is that some Republicans will use mentoring as a smoke screen to cover up cutbacks

> *"What we're trying to do is to put a sufficient number of older volunteers in schools so that they could actually change the environment so that they became essentially mentor-rich environments. And, in the process, to try to rebuild the constituency for public schools among neighborhood elders who are a greater and greater share of the population."*

to really basic youth services in schools and things of that sort. And that is something that we have to be—and I'm always—wary of.

BB: One point I just loved in your document and book and that totally strikes home with me since I'm concerned with restructuring systems like schools, communities, and organizations is that the real issue is how we create *mentor-rich environments* where there are lots of opportunities for young people to interact with lots of adults, where that kind of chemistry can happen in a natural sort of way. This is what Emmy [Werner] refers to when she talks about the key to successful prevention is to create the natural social networks where things aren't so much programs but that you are really supporting the natural connections between friends, family, neighbors, young and old, etc.—by having enough people in kids' lives in the institutions they are in.

MF: There are two arguments for that. One is the number of children that we can reach. I mean there are profound limits on the young people that can be reached in the way that Big Brothers and Big Sisters goes about it. After 100 years, there are 75,000 people in Big Brothers/Big Sisters and half as many people on the waiting list. Dagmar McGill, the Associate National Director of Big Brothers/Big Sisters, estimates that between 5 and 15 million kids could benefit from what they provide. Well there's a big gulf between 75,000 and 5 to 15 million.

So then the question is, how could we reach more of those kids? One way is through Americorps and Foster Grandparents or National Service participants who have the spirit of volunteerism but are working half-to- full-time so they can reach multiple kids. And another route is to try to figure out where young people are spending their time, and to try to see how those institutions, namely schools and community youth programs, could be changed so they become opportunities for more relationships to form with both volunteers and staff.

The project I'm working on now is the Experience Corps, which is in many ways an attempt to build mentor-rich environments in urban elementary schools and inner city neighborhoods (in the South Bronx, Philadelphia, Minneapolis, Portland, Oregon, and Port Arthur, Texas). One of the things that I learned from studying mentoring, and is confirmed by the Big Brother/Big Sister study, is that while it's incredibly important for kids to have mentors, the big issue is to have mentors who can put in a sufficient amount of time to form real relationships. We know that the segment in society who has the most time at this juncture are retirees. So this project is an attempt to not only create mentor-rich environments in the schools but to mobilize essentially the group in society which has the time to provide this kind of relation.

In the past, older adults have been involved in working in schools in a variety of ways, but they tend to be peripheral roles. What we're trying to do is to put a sufficient number of older volunteers in schools so that they could actually change the environment so that they became essentially mentor-rich environments. And, in the process, to try to rebuild the constituency for public schools among neighborhood elders who are a greater and greater share of the population.

BB: Something you've pointed out, as well as others like Ron Ferguson's research at the JFK School of Public Policy at Harvard, is that it's often the *case manager or youth worker* that actually is playing the real mentoring role. I think that the "I Have a Dream" mentoring study also found something like that. This seems to have some real profound implications: If we can support more community-based youth-serving programs—and the youth worker staff—or support teachers in schools by reducing class size or making sure all schools have counselors or bringing in volunteers into these institutions, we can make a real difference. It seems like this type of restructuring—supporting youth workers, teachers, counselors, etc. that are natural mentors—is just not as "sexy" as volunteer mentoring programs.

> *"I think that people have a hard time realizing that mentoring is not the exclusive province of volunteers. But what we know from real life is that most mentoring relationships form in the context of work or school—a teacher and a student, a coach and an athlete, an employer and employee."*

MF: I think that people have a hard time realizing that mentoring is not the exclusive province of volunteers. Groups like Big Brothers/Big Sisters which have been around for so long and are so widely known have defined the mentoring movement so much that people assume it has to be something that is a voluntary activity. But what we know from real life is that *most mentoring relationships form in the context of work or school—a teacher and a student, a coach and an athlete, an employer and employee.* Most real mentoring does occur between people who are in paid positions working on something.

The main problem is just that we have identified mentoring so exclusively with Big Brothers/Big Sisters that we don't realize that there are a lot of others already spending an enormous amount of time with young people and who are naturally in a strong position to form those kinds of relationships—these are people like teachers and coaches and youth workers. In many ways they are in a better position to reach a wide number of young people.

BB: Somehow we can't seem to muster the political will to get us interested in promoting youth development. People ask me when we talk about youth development, do you think we should just get rid of the term "prevention"? People like Karen Pittman think that we probably should. My concern is, would we have *any* dollars spent for youth programming if people weren't afraid of the problems—like substance abuse, violence, etc.—that youth can present?

MF: We've gotten to the point where fear is the principle motivator—and it's not a very good motivator. It's a lot easier for people to retreat than it is for them to act. So there's much more of the trend towards disengagement than there is toward reengaging in programs like BB/BS. It's easier to move to the suburbs or some walled community. The number one growing occupation in the U.S. is security guards.

BB: And the number one growth industry in California is prisons. And the ironic and sad thing about it all is that people go into those walled communities and kind of numb themselves on TV, work, or drugs, when reengaging with especially young people could give them a sense that their life had meaning. What advice would you offer the prevention field?

MF: I would go back to the subject that we talked about earlier. At the same time that substance abuse among teenagers is doubling, we've shown pretty systematically that these kinds of relationships can produce exactly the opposite trend. What is so striking is that these were not professional substance abuse counselors. These were not people who were focusing on the problems of youth. All they were were people who just wanted to be friends with young people—the ones who were most effective. *I think it just highlights how much we need to get back to the basics of what kids need, and that will not only improve their immediate quality of life by providing caring relationships with adults, but probably prove to be a more effective vehicle for preventing problem behaviors.* ➤

Marc Freedman is president of an organization he has recently founded in Berkeley, CA, called Civic Ventures, whose focus is on "expanding the contribution of older Americans to society, and particularly to kids." He can be reached there at (510) 540-4896.

Juanita Corriz: A Relationship with a Big Sister Taught Her to"Want Everything There is Good For Me in Life"

by Nan Henderson, M.S.W.

Too often, programs fostering resiliency and positive youth development have only case example data or only quantified data to show their effectiveness. Big Brothers/Big Sisters of America offers both, providing the only large-scale study to date quantifying the effectiveness of their structured approach to mentoring, as well as countless case examples of the resiliency-fostering effects of this program in the lives of individual youth. Juanita Corriz is one such example. In a recent interview, she added a wildly enthusiastic face of resiliency to the quantitative data also included in this book, as she talked about her Big Sister, Sharyn Obsatz, and about what their relationship has done for her.

Juanita Corriz is a 15-year-old in Santa Fe, New Mexico with a focus: "I want to graduate, to get my education done, to think for myself, and to stay out of trouble." She also sees herself as a role model for her three younger brothers and sisters. "I want people to look up to me in my family. Like my brothers and sisters... that's what I'm trying to do, I'm the oldest and I have three young ones looking up to me, you know. And if I can do it, hopefully, they'll want to do it , too."

Juanita has made a decision to have a different life than her mother, who dropped out of high school at 17 "with only two credits left" to have a baby. Juanita's father had left; he "was promised to marry another woman," she explained. "My mom was disappointed but she knew she could make it, just me and her, on her own. I also have two brothers and one sister," she added. Her mother relied on welfare and food stamps to support her four children until Juanita was 10. Then she went to work as a night custodian at the State Capitol. Juanita has seen her father only twice in her entire life, and credits her mom for doing "her best to raise us... she's always been there for us, and she's been our strength to carry into life."

Juanita said her mom set an example for her by getting off welfare, going to work, "trying to make it." And her mother also helped her by encouraging her to stay in school and learn from her mistakes, to try to "become something better for myself." One of the best things Juanita's mother did was to initiate contact with Big Brothers/Big Sisters of Santa Fe when Juanita was 12.

Juanita eagerly reported that she had a 3.0 in school last year and is working to get at least one 4.0 this year. "I'm going to try to do good because I know I can do good," she said. When asked how she developed that understanding, Juanita said that she learned it, "Pretty much from my Big Sister, Sharyn." After being on the Big Brothers/Big Sisters waiting list for two years, Juanita was matched with Sharyn Obsatz, a Minnesota native who became the county reporter for the Santa Fe newspaper, *The New Mexican*, in 1994.

Juanita explained the process: A caseworker from the program "came up to my house and interviewed me by myself, asked me questions like what I like to do and what are my favorite things…to match me and another person for what we like to do. And they compared my paper and Sharyn's paper, and they saw that we had a lot of similarities, so that's how they make the match." She added, "Me and Sharyn met, and we hit it off!"

Juanita Corriz and her Big Sister, Sharyn Obsatz

Juanita said that she and Sharyn do all kinds of fun activities together. "The first time we hung out together, we went hiking and just talked. And since then we've taken dance lessons…we go out to eat…sometimes we have sleepovers. We do our nails and watch T.V. and pig out. Then we've had times where we just go and sit under a tree and read for awhile."

Their bond has grown far beyond just having fun together. "She made such a big difference for me because my mom sometimes…with four of us hardly has time to spend with all of us individually. But I have Sharyn as a best friend… to become very close to me. I've grown to love her, and we understand each other. Like, if anything happened, she was there for me. She's just been there for me in hard times and good times. She's just very understanding. I hope we stay paired until I graduate."

Sharyn, Juanita said, has been a role model and a mentor for going on to college. Sharyn asks her about school every weekend and is available to call for help on homework during the week. And she gives Juanita this message: "She knows I can do it, that I'm very smart, to get a good education, and to try the best I can. And she's trying to get me to read more; she likes to read," Juanita added.

But on Fridays, it is the fun they will have together Juanita anticipates. "Without Sharyn, the weekends would be more boring. I wouldn't really look forward to the weekends. [Now], I get happy, you know, on Fridays, when I'm going to hang out with my Big Sister and see her and talk to her… [tell] her what happened at school, and stuff. I feel if I hadn't met her, school would probably be harder for me because Sharyn is somebody I look up to, you know. If I hadn't had Sharyn, I would have had nobody to really look up to, or to care about my grades—other than my mom—to really push me to doing the best I can do knowing I can do it."

She adds that having Sharyn in her life helps her stay out of trouble. "If it wasn't for my Big Sister, I would probably have an attitude like my cousins, you know, who say that nobody else is doing it, so just drop out, and who cares about school. But I'm doing good, and kids my age aren't usually doing good these days. I want to get everything there is good for me in life."

Juanita said she thinks about being an interpreter after attending college. "I know how to speak Spanish real good and English. And I'll be taking French. So, I'll know three languages, and then I [want to] get in two more languages."

And she has a vision of herself in three years as the second of "about 20 cousins" to graduate from high school. "I want people to look at me and say, 'Wow! Juanita did it. Good for her! She deserves a lot in life because she tried her hardest to make something of herself.'" Her vision of her future includes becoming a Big Sister herself one day. "I would like to come back to Santa Fe after college and be a Big Sister here because I've seen the way it helped me. Hopefully, I can help somebody else." ➤

Nan Henderson, M.S.W., is a national speaker and consultant on fostering resiliency and wellness, alcohol and other drug issues, and on organizational change. She has coauthored/edited five books about resiliency, and is the Editor-in-chief at Resiliency In Action, Inc. She can be reached at Nan Henderson and Associates, 5130 La Jolla Blvd., #2K, San Diego, CA 92109, p/f (858-488-5034), or by e-mail: (nanh@connectnet.com).

The Politics of Mentoring: What Must Happen for It to Really Work

by Marc Freedman, M.A.

Marc Freedman is the author of the book The Kindness of Strangers: Reflections on the Mentoring Movement. *Published in 1992, this book is considered the most comprehensive and critical look at the mentoring movement that has been published. Working with the research organization Public/Private Ventures (PPV), Marc was instrumental in the study of Big Brothers/Big Sisters which PPV undertook in the early 1990s. His comments below are excerpted from a presentation on mentoring that he gave at the 1998 Conference on Resiliency In Action, held February 19 and 20 in San Diego, CA.*

It's become increasingly difficult for young people in market societies to have much sustained contact with adults who care about them. I think it's occurring in every sphere of life. The statistics about families are familiar: one out of four children is born into a single parent household, more than half of the African American children in the country [are] born into a single parent household, 40% of the kids in the country have no contacts with their father, there's been a doubling of one-parent households since the 1980s, and on and on. People are working pretty hard. As Juliet Schor, an economist from Harvard, wrote about five years ago, there's been a 164- hour increase in the number of hours that the average American works each year. So people are working an extra month—13 months in a space of 12—and much of that time is coming from time spent with children. It is not just in families where big changes have taken place. Neighborhoods, an important source of informal support for kids, have themselves become impersonal places. A recent J. Walter Thompson study showed that three out of four Americans don't know the person living next door, and in many low income neighborhoods, a threat of community violence ends up driving [people] behind barred doors.

> "So [when kids] need [adult] support most, [when] they're under the most stress, they're getting it least from the places where [it has been] in the past."

It's becoming more difficult for a lot of the informal contact that occurred in the past to take place. And the institution that could potentially compensate for that, school, is itself often more a part of the problem than the solution. In schools in San Francisco, the student-counselor ratio at the elementary level is 600 to 1, in New York City it's over 1,000 to 1. Teachers have classes of 30 to 40 students and in many places around the country, it's not uncommon for a teacher to see 200 faces in a day. So even the most caring teachers often find it hard to connect with more than a couple of the kids they are teaching.

At the same time there are fewer and fewer adults in the places where adults used to be available for kids, it's become a lot harder to be a kid. In a recent study of six inner-city neighborhoods, 30% of the kids by the age of 15 had actually watched somebody being shot, while 70% had seen somebody being beaten. Another study by Louis Harris and Associates of 2,000 teenagers found that one in eight young people carries a weapon to school for protection, and in high crime areas the number jumps to almost two in five. Young people cut classes or stay away from school regularly out of fear for their safety. So [when kids] need [adult] support the most, [when] they're under the most stress, they're getting it least from the places where [it has been] in the past. And that [is] not only something we should feel uncomfortable or concerned about, it is [also] a missed opportunity [for adults].

> *"The mystery [the researchers] were trying to unravel is why some neighborhoods have high rates of community violence and other neighborhoods have much lower rates."*

Many Studies Show the Power of a Mentor

Two anthropologists [at] City University of New York and NYU studied 900 kids in rural Mississippi and a medium-sized city like Louisville and [in] New York City and [concluded that] the difference between the kids who made it and [those who] didn't was the presence or absence of an adult mentor. Just last year Arthur Levine, the Dean of Teachers College at Columbia University, did a set of case studies of 24 young people who made it out of poverty to Ivy League universities. The common denominator again was the presence of a caring adult, an unrelated adult who would come into their lives and provide important critical assistance.

There were two other studies that came out over the past year which I think are absolutely staggering. The biggest study ever done of community violence in America of neighborhoods in Chicago, low income neighborhoods with identical demographic circumstances, [was published]. The mystery [the researchers] were trying to unravel is why some neighborhoods have high rates of community violence and other neighborhoods have much lower rates. In some neighborhoods adults took significant interest in the lives of young people, particularly [those] who were screwing up, doing graffiti, and cutting school. In those neighborhoods, adults took it upon themselves to intervene and the difference was [a huge reduction] in community violence. The other really staggering study was the biggest study of adolescents in America ever done, 90,000 teenagers. The principle researcher, Robert Blum from the University of Minnesota, [said] in the *New York Times* that families invest an enormous amount of energy in rules and regulations for kids, but that's not where the action is. The action is in adults connecting with kids. That article was published in the *Journal of the American Medical Association* [September 10, 1997].

When you actually sit down and read Emmy [Werner's] work or other work on resilience, [you find that] these kids succeed because they had mentors—and that they had mentors because they were resilient. They recruited the mentors, they basically presented themselves at the mentor's doorstep and instructed the mentor that they would be mentoring them. They have this extraordinary ability to recruit adults to take a special interest in them. [The resilience research] is suggestive, but inconclusive. Fortunately over the last few years, there have been a series of studies that have brought us much closer to understanding the mystery [of resilience] that have also turned out to be enormously encouraging.

One small study was done by Jean Rhodes, a clinical psychologist at the University of Illinois, who spent two years studying girls at the Simpson Alternative School in Chicago, a school for teenage moms. She first looked at the natural mentors who existed in the lives of these girls, and the big surprise was that there were a lot of natural mentors in the girls' lives. They turned out to be the sister of the mother of the father of the child in most cases, which is kind of an interesting finding in and of itself. So basically [it was] their aunt from the father's side, a person who had a blood interest in the child, but wasn't as connected as the mother.

Persistence is a Key Finding

What Jean came up with is two groups of girls, ones who had natural mentors and ones who had no mentors in their lives. Then she assigned unique "sisters" to half of the girls in each group. So [she] had four different groups: girls with natural and Big Sister-type mentors, girls with neither, and girls with one or the other. Jean came up with two findings: First, the rich do in fact get richer. The girls who had natural mentors ended up being spectacularly good at using these Big Sister-type mentors; a very high proportion of those turned into strong relationships. But a significant number of girls who had no natural mentors were able to form relationships with these Big Sisters, and *the difference in every single case that she studied was persistence on the part of the mentors.* They were the ones who just kept showing up despite lack of early interest on the part of the kid, [or] lack of phone calls being returned. Persistence ended up being

> *"The difference in every single case …was persistence on the part of the mentors. [This] ended up being the key variable in reaching kids who didn't have the natural ability to just win over adults easily."*

the key variable in reaching the kids who didn't presumably have that natural ability to just win adults over easily. That was really encouraging. But it was with a small number of girls, all teenage moms who one would assume were particularly receptive to having relationships with adults at a really stressful time of their lives. What about the rest of the world?

In 1992, Public/Private Ventures, the organization I worked with, saw a great fundraising opportunity in "the rest of the world," so we ended up raising a couple of million dollars to study the Big Brothers/Big Sisters Program. They were willing to evaluate after almost 75 years for one simple reason: All these other mentoring programs were popping up saying they could do a better job at a fraction of the cost, and United Way, the principle funding source of Big Brothers/Big Sisters, started to [ask] why they should pay all this money when [this is available elsewhere] for half the cost. So in the beginning of 1992, we studied 1,000 kids who applied to be in the Big Brothers/Big Sisters Program. It was a random assignment, control group study in which we were able to study 500 kids who got Big Brothers and Big Sisters, and 500 kids who didn't (because the average length of time on the waiting list of the [program] is 18 months). Then after 18 months, we [evaluated] what happened.

Can Social Science Research Measure Relationships?

I was very worried about this study. I felt the vast majority of good things that were happening were too subtle to ever show up on a meek social science study of [this] type. I went to the Oakland Big Brothers/Big Sisters Program quite a bit and I remember one mentor telling me the story of a kid he was working with: For the first two or three months of the program, the mentor would decide every week what they would do. They'd go to the zoo this weekend, the next weekend to the ball game, and the next week they would do something else. He decided that it was too one-sided and wanted [his Little Brother] to take the more active role in the relationship. So [he] informed the Little Brother that the next time they got together it would be up to the kid to decide what they were going to do. Anything the boy wanted to do within reason they would do that day. So he showed up that following Saturday at the kid's house and said, "What are we doing today?" After about 20 minutes of stone silence, he said, "This is ridiculous, we only have a chance to get together once a week, we're going to waste the whole day. What do you want us to do?" Finally, after another few minutes of ducking the issue, the kid said, "I want to go to your house." By this point the mentor was really frustrated, he lives all the way on the other side of town. [But] they got into the car and drove over to his house. And the whole process repeated itself. They sat in the car about 10-15 minutes. Now the Big Brother was getting visibly disturbed by all this. Finally the young person admitted that what he wanted to do was see this guy shave, because he had never seen a man shave in his entire life. What could be more important in terms of becoming an adult than to do things like that?

> *"First, this study [showed] that it is possible to do something as delicate as create a human relationship in the context of the social program. That in and of itself is really important. But more than that, we found that you don't have to be a charismatic superhero to form that relationship."*

So I was worried that [in this] really expensive social science study all that stuff was going to be missed. In fact, the exact opposite was true. The results of the study were staggering. There was a 46% difference in kids starting to use drugs between kids who had mentors, Big Brothers and Big Sisters, and kids who didn't, a 70% difference for African American boys, and a huge difference in starting to use alcohol. All the biggest gains were in juvenile justice-related areas: a 33% [reduction] in violent behavior, 50% [reduction] in school truancy [for the kids who had the mentors compared to the control group who did not].

There were big differences in behavior [and] attitudes. These kids got along much better with their parents as a result of being in the program, much more of an attitude [finding]. They did better in school. All the changes pointed in the same direction. And these weren't a bunch of rich kids from the suburbs. It turned out that 60% of the sample was a member of a minority, mostly African American; 80% came from impoverished families; and almost all were being raised by a single parent, usually the mother. [In addition], 40% were from homes with a history of drug or alcohol abuse, and nearly 30% came from histories of domestic violence. So these kids were facing a lot and [having the mentor made] a huge difference.

But even more significant [were the findings from looking at what] kinds of relationships matter, in terms of actually putting into operation why some mentors did better and some of the programs did better than others. Here, [too], the differences were really staggering. First, this study [showed] that it is possible to do something as delicate as create a human relationship in the context of the social program. That in and of itself is really important. But more than that, we found that you don't have to be a charismatic superhero to form that relationship. [See chapters one and two for more details about the Big Brothers/Big Sisters study.]

Two Things are Necessary for Good Mentoring

That's one of the main criticisms of mentoring, [this attitude of] "oh well, anybody who's fantastic with kids is going to be able to do this, but what about the average person?" It turns out that you've [basically] got to do two things to be a really good mentor. One thing is that you have to show up. The Big Brothers/Big Sisters Program [mentors] put ten and a half hours a month into the program. But the interesting finding here is that these relationships have a life of their own and it doesn't matter so much the rule of the program. It turns out that some Big Brothers/Big Sisters Programs require the traditional four meetings a month, and other programs try to liberalize that to get more people into the program. [However], regardless of whether there are two or

> *"It turns out that you've [basically] got to do two things to be a really good mentor ... show up... put in the time— consistent time. That is a critical variable. The other part, which is just as critical, is that you have to become not [so] concerned about making a difference. There's a paradox [here]."*

> *"There are about 50 million kids estimated who could use the benefits of the mentor, and there are probably about 300,000 volunteer mentors in the country."*

four meetings [a month required by the program], people show up [an average of] 3.1 times a month. It doesn't really matter what the program says. And they show up for about three and a half hours a time. So you have to put in the time—consistent time. That's a critical variable.

The other part, which is just as critical, is that you have to become not [so] concerned about making a difference. There's a basic paradox [here] and I think this was the most staggering of all of the findings. We found that there were two types of relationships, [which we called] "developmental" and "prescriptive". The

developmental relationships have mentors who take the approach [of] involving young people in deciding how the pair will spend their time together. They make a commitment to be consistent and dependable. They recognize that the relationship may be fairly one-sided for some time—it may involve silence and unresponsiveness from the young person—[but] the adult takes the responsibility for keeping the relationship alive. They [also] pay attention—this is very important—to

> *"It turns out that the best way to make a difference with kids is to just try to have a real relationship and have fun."*

youths' needs for fun. Not only is having fun a key part of the relationship building, but it provides valuable opportunities that are often not otherwise available to the [kids]. They [also] respect the young person's viewpoint. But having fun was the thing we kept coming back to [and] the people who were trying to have fun [were the ones] who made this huge difference. After nine months, 91% of those [developmental] relationships were still meeting regularly.

After nine months the other types of relationships, [the prescriptive relationships] where people were trying to save kids, only 30% of those relationships were meeting regularly. The prescriptive mentors attempted to transform or reform the youth by setting goals early on and adopting a parental or authoritative role in their interactions with youth. They emphasized behavior change more. They had difficulty meeting with youth on a regular and consistent basis. They attempted to instill a set of values that [were] different from or inconsistent with those the youth expected at home. And they ignored advise of program staff.

It turns out that the best way to make a difference with kids is to just try to have a real relationship and have fun. These were really basically a form of love relationships [with] real bonding and attachment. Those were the people who made a huge difference in the lives of kids.

[It also] turns out that matching actually mattered. Some programs like Big Brothers/Big Sisters, for instance, have really

> *"My estimate is that we need about a billion and a half dollars to come anywhere near trying to close that gap of 50 million kids."*

terrific staff support, case workers, follow-up, and do lots of screening and training. They weed out the people who aren't prepared to be persistent or who have the wrong approach to mentoring. They find the right kinds of people and stick with them and they [provide these mentors] somebody to turn to. But it turns out that all these characteristics didn't matter nearly so much as basically people showing up and trying to have a good time and a real relationship with kids.

Mentors Needed for 50 Million or More

The main problem is that there are about 50 million kids estimated who could use the benefits of a mentor, and there are probably about 300,000 volunteer mentors in the country. So there's this vast abiding gap between the number of kids who could benefit from this—and probably that number is much greater than 50 million—and the number of volunteers. Big Brothers/Big Sisters alone is a start. There are 75,000 kids being matched in that program. As I said before, [they have a] waiting list of 18 months. There are 30,000 kids on the waiting list [primarily] African American boys. For every 100 Caucasian boys, for example, on the Big Brothers/Big Sisters waiting list, there are 100 in the program. For every 100 on the waiting list who are African American boys, only 65 [are] in the program. So there's a big gap even in that program and they've been around for 100 years. They've been trying to recruit more, and they're not making much progress.

> *"[At] the presidential summit last year, people were talking about 2 million mentors by the year 2000. If Big Brothers/ Big Sisters has gotten [only] 75,000 after nearly 100 years, where are the other 1,925,000 people going to come from over the next one year and ten months from now?"*

That's all the more startling in the context of the presidential summit last year where people were talking about 2 million mentors by the year 2000. I want to figure [this] out: If Big Brothers/ Big Sisters has gotten [only] 75,000 after nearly 100 years, where are the other 1,925,000 people going to come from over the next one year and ten months? [It is a] big problem finding adults who will do this. In the Big Brothers/Big Sisters Program, for example, [for] every 100 people who approach the program, only 20 are actually placed with kids. So there's a big problem finding adults.

There's a basic paradox that the mentor volunteer movement rests on: Adults get excited about it [because] they recognize that men and women in society are not spending enough time with kids. Unfortunately, they don't have enough time to spend with their own kids. So where can we find 925,000 people to spend $10^{1}/_{2}$ hours a month with somebody else's kids? I think we are overlooking the one great untapped resource for kids in this country, retired people. There are now 30 million Americans over the age of 65 and by the year 2020 that number is going to double to over 60 million. A quarter of the population is going to be over the age of 65. It's kind of ironic that the mentoring movement has focused on the people in the society who have the least time, and ignored the group in society who has the most time. And time is everything in mentoring. It's not just that people can be consistent when they have more time, but it really leads to the kind of attitude, perspective, and patience that are closely associated with the successful relationships.

The other [issue] is that there's a money problem. Big Brothers/ Big Sisters costs a $1,000 a match—all that screening, training, follow-ups, support. That's too expensive. But even if we assume $500 a match we've got to figure out a way to come up with more money to do this responsibly. My estimate is that we need about a billion and a half dollars to come anywhere near trying to close that gap of 50 million kids. We've got to find more people to do it and we've got to find the money to make that happen in a responsible way.

> *"There's been too much focus on volunteer mentoring as the exclusive way to reach kids. We need to recreate social work roles and other kinds of staff roles [so] that people have more time to spend with kids, and are freed up from all the paperwork."*

When I went out and visited a bunch of mentoring programs, not [just] Big Brothers/Big Sisters, one of the things I found was that a lot of the mentoring that was occurring in programs [was] actually being done by the staff, not the volunteers. I went to a project in Baltimore [at] an elementary school. When I got to the school I was looking for the program director, a social worker, and found that his office was in a broom closet in the school. [I also found] a line about half way down the corridor of kids who were just waiting to talk to him, because he was somebody who was there day-in and day-out. [He wasn't] downtown in some fancy office behind a secretary. He wasn't in Phoenix on business. He was somebody who showed up at the school everyday, day-in and day-out. Talk about persistence. [See chapters seven and nine for other examples of this type of mentoring.]

One Solution: Creating Mentor-Rich Institutions

I think there's been too much focus on volunteer mentoring as the exclusive way to reach kids. We need to recreate social work roles and other kinds of staff roles [so] that people have more time to spend with kids, and are freed up from all the paperwork. I think some of the most important implications of mentoring are not just what volunteers can do or even staff, but how we need to transform our institutions for kids in the non-school hours so that relationship is a much more central objective of how they do their business. Ultimately, the solution is to create mentor-rich environments for kids. I think that's one of the most radical implications, the idea of creating these mentor-rich environments. You know that's going to cost a lot of money.

But I throw out one thread of hope: In all the interviews I've done with mentors, one of the things I've discovered is mentoring is every bit as much of a social program for adults as it is for kids. We tend to focus on how isolated kids are from contact with adults—all the statistics I [mentioned] before. But the mentors I've talked to have never experienced anybody in a relationship [like that] young person from a different neighborhood, from a different socioeconomic group, and they learn certainly as much as the kids. One of the things they learn is that these kids aren't that different from their own kids. And they starting asking the very disturbing question: How would I do under these circumstances, how would my kids do? For these mentors what was happening to these kids was not some impersonal statistic, but something that was hitting home. I think there's great potential in building a constituency for kids in bringing together people who will have had similar experiences, and [are] often in a position to lobby for changes in education and so forth.

So for all these reasons—what mentoring can do for young people directly, what it can do for the adults involved, for some of the broader institutional implications, for its potential to build a constituency for young people at time when one hardly exists—I think this whole movement is a window of hope.

I still worry, [though]. I've been seeing a lot of commercials for mentoring on TV, and I'm wondering, "Where is the investment in the programs so that when people show up they actually are able to use their time well and have a good experience?" One of the things that is even more shocking for me is that all these retired presidents and General Powell, all these retirees, are telling [us that we] should be more for kids. What they really should be doing is talking to their peers—the one group that has the time to do this. They should say [to them], "It's time." ➤

> **"Mentoring is every bit as much of a social program for adults as it is for kids."**

Marc Freedman is president of an organization he has recently founded in Berkeley, CA, called Civic Ventures, whose focus is on "expanding the contribution of older Americans to society, and particularly to kids." He can be reached there at (510) 540-4896.

MARCH Provides Boys with the Support, Knowledge, and Skills to Become Healthy Men

by Susanne Reno

This chapter is reprinted with permission from the December 1997 Educator's Update, *a bimonthly newsletter published by Planned Parenthood Federation of America, Inc.*

Adolescent pregnancy prevention programs have often focused on young women. Obviously, to have an impact on teen pregnancy, males must be included in these efforts. The challenge is to develop programs that will involve, not alienate, young men. With this shift toward male involvement, Planned Parenthood of San Diego and Riverside Counties (PPSDRC) saw an opportunity to create a male-centered approach to sexuality education that would focus on the positive and healthy aspects of being a man.

PPSDRC's education and training department received a grant from the San Diego Foundation to develop and implement the Males Acting Responsibly for Community Health (MARCH) Program. The amount received (approximately $66,000) was less than originally requested, but it provided an opportunity to develop a pilot program. PPSDRC could conduct focus groups, assess community needs, and hire an evaluator to ensure the development of an effective program.

Getting Started: Assessing Existing Programs for Boys and Young Men

It was important not to duplicate community efforts, so PPSDRC hosted a luncheon for the community agencies [in San Diego] that were working with men. We found that although these agencies had been providing services to young men, mostly teen fathers, they had no provision for collecting and evaluating their programs. Additionally, we learned that all of these agencies were targeting men ages 14-25, and that most of these men reported they had already engaged in sexual intercourse or were teen fathers. None of the agencies we talked with focused on boys before they engaged in intercourse or became fathers. The need was for prevention, and for us, that meant working with younger boys.

PPSDRC decided that the target audience for MARCH would be males ages 11-12, who resided in zip code areas with high rates of teen pregnancy and gang violence. This age group was selected because the participants would be in sixth grade, and according to the "Youth Risk Behavior Survey" funded by the Centers for Disease Control and San Diego Unified Schools, there is a sharp increase in risk behavior among youth after starting junior high. Therefore, we wanted to provide these young men with the skills that would assist them as they got to junior high and were faced with greater pressures to engage in high risk behaviors.

The overall goal of MARCH is to increase young men's awareness of their role and responsibilities in relation to teen pregnancy prevention, sexually transmitted disease prevention, and relationship violence prevention. MARCH activities are designed to build self-esteem, to bring purpose to the young men's lives, and to establish and set life goals. Additionally, male educators serve as role models to achieve these goals.

Using Focus Groups of Boys to Learn How to Design MARCH

Focus groups were conducted to identify attitudes about relationships, gender roles, community involvement, and gaps in knowledge about sexuality. Focus groups were important, not only for curriculum development, but also to learn what would motivate an 11 or 12-year-old boy to attend a 14-week, after-school session provided by Planned Parenthood. We learned that these young men wanted sporting equipment (e.g., basketballs and soccer balls), and they wanted the program to be interactive and activity oriented. So the program was developed based on Planned Parenthood goals and what they wanted.

MARCH program participants visit the tide pools at the Cabrillo Monument in San Diego.

"Most of the boys haven't been to local San Diego attractions like Cabrillo, even though they were born and raised here."

We collaborated with four elementary schools located within the previously identified zip codes. The counselors, nurses, and principles at these schools provided boys who they felt could "go either way." Many of the participants' siblings were teen parents and/or involved in gangs, so the school administrators felt that these were young men who were particularly at risk [for similar involvement]. Participants were required to have parental permission, and participation in the MARCH program was voluntary. We requested that the schools keep the ethnicity of their schools in mind when looking for participants to ensure that each group reflected the diversity of that school. The groups that developed were about 40% Latino/Hispanic, 30% African American, 20% Caucasian, 5% Asian, and 5% from other backgrounds.

Thirty-seven boys in four groups spent 14 weeks (28 hours of education) discussing healthy relationships, self-esteem, gender roles, puberty, and making healthy choices. Games were designed and used to develop team building, conflict resolution, and analytical skills. Additionally, since building pride in their community was important, they also participated in community service programs (e.g., cleaning vacant lots and painting over graffiti).

Evaluating the Participants and Evaluating the Program

At the conclusion of each session a Peer Behavior Assessment (1-5 scale) was completed for each participant. Because each young man assisted in behavior assessment, they had an opportunity to role model positive peer pressure. This instilled a sense of connection to the group and illustrated how their individual behavior had an effect, either positive or negative, on the group. If participants disagreed with the points that they received, the participants had the opportunity to practice their conflict resolution, negotiation, and assertiveness skills. Points were also given for perfect attendance and for positive participation. At the end of the 14 weeks, points were totaled to determine honor graduates. Honor graduates received special recognition and additional rewards (e.g., trophies and movie tickets) at the MARCH commencement ceremony. Each MARCH participant was also provided with a MARCH t-shirt that had been designed by the participants.

At the conclusion of the pilot year, the program evaluation indicated that MARCH did impact attitudes and intentions to reduce relationship violence and increase prosocial behaviors. The greatest impact appeared to be in the areas of sexually transmitted diseases and teen pregnancy prevention and knowledge of resources related to puberty and adolescent health. In addition, the role play evaluation indicated an increase in decision-making skills related to negotiation, peer pressure, and active listening skills.

Followup to the Pilot Program

The evaluation results were very encouraging and showed us that we were on the right track. Armed with the evaluation of the MARCH pilot program, PPSDRC has approached two foundations to obtain additional funding and we are optimistic about receiving more support. The additional funding will be used to expand MARCH to 10 schools and 300 participants, and to implement a similar pilot program for girls ages 11 and 12.

An important component of the MARCH program was to provide the boys with a place to go after they graduated from the program. This was accomplished by collaborating with Smart Teens Education Peers (STEP) program and the Circulo de Hombres program through a community agency located in the targeted zip code area. STEP focuses on males ages 13-19 and Circulo de Hombres works with men ages 19 and up. Boys that graduate from the MARCH program are referred and can use the knowledge gained from MARCH to continue in the capacity of peer educators.

Lessons Learned from the Pilot Program

Young men are willing to address these issues. Even though it was important to the participants to have tangible rewards, they still gave up their after-school time for an entire semester to discuss relationships and sex. It is the responsibility of sexuality educators to welcome young men and involve them.

The program participants are the best marketing tool. When asked to present at a Planned Parenthood board meeting and at a meeting with funders, I invited a few

MARCH participants to share their experience of the program. Nothing sells a program better than the people receiving the service.

Start small. Using the data obtained from the pilot program, we were able to approach funders with some "hard data" showing that we were on the right track. Additionally, because we were attempting to implement a program from the ground up (e.g., focus groups, needs assessment, and evaluation) it was important to start small and have a solid success with which to approach funders.

Understand the importance of the staff. We focused on hiring men who had similar backgrounds as the program participants. Part of these men's responsibility was to be positive role models and mentors. They had to be familiar with the community and be willing to attend school functions; they needed to be visible and approachable.

Don't skimp on evaluation. Foundations love evaluation and it is easy to sell the idea with it, thus justifying to them their expenditure of money. With a solid evaluation piece, chances are the funding amounts will increase to cover this cost.

Collaborate with other agencies in the area. This gave us an entree into the community and increased our credibility. Communities are mistrustful of agencies [and programs] that come and go, so teaming up with another trusted community agency helped to alleviate this concern. ◄

Update on MARCH: Additional Funding Expands
the Program to Reach More Boys *and* Girls

MARCH has come a long way in its short existence. Initiated with funding from Blue Cross Community Clinics Fund of the San Diego Foundation, MARCH served 37 boys in its pilot phase. Its next stage of expansion has recently been awarded a significant grant from the Alliance Healthcare Foundation.

The grant will support outreach to approximately 300 sixth grade boys and 300 sixth grade girls in 10 San Diego city schools. Focus groups for the girls' program [began] in June and will be followed by a pilot study to begin in the fall.

Alliance Healthcare is a San Diego foundation focusing on the health care needs of medically indigent and under-served populations primarily in San Diego County. Additional grant support has been received from the Blue Cross Clinics Fund, the Favrot Fund, the Blair Family Discretionary Fund, the Helen and Howard Goldfeder Discretionary Fund, and The General Discretionary Fund of the San Diego Foundation.

An after-school program spanning 13 weeks [due to modifications after the pilot program of 14 weeks], MARCH educates boys ages 11 to 12 in life skills, respectful relationships, goal-setting, and decision-making. Intending to reach them before they engage in sexual activity or become fathers, MARCH emphasizes a whole person experience and guides the boys in skill development that will help them set and achieve their goals.

Reprinted with permission from the spring 1998 issue of Choice Words, *a publication of Planned Parenthood of San Diego and Riverside Counties.*

Susanne Reno is Vice President of Education and Training for Planned Parenthood of San Diego and Riverside Counties. She can be reached by phone (619-683-7545, ext. 174) or by e-mail (susanne_reno@PPFA.org).

A Self-Esteem Approach to Effective Resiliency Building: The Process of Mentoring

by Ralph Renger, Ph.D., Pamela Kalbfleisch, Ph.D.,
Linda Smolak, Ph.D., Marjorie Crago, Ph.D.

Low self-esteem is a common denominator among many youth with behavioral and emotional problems. Youth suffering from depression, eating disorders, academic failure, delinquent behavior, and substance abuse all are characterized as having low self-esteem (Button, Sonuga-Barke, Davies, & Thompson, 1996; Dubois, Felner, Sherman, & Bull, 1994; Jessor, 1993; Seligman, 1995; Shisslak, Crago, Estes, & Gray, 1996; Turner, Norman, & Zunz, 1995).

Another common denominator among youth diagnosed with the above disorders is the absence of a caring adult (American Psychiatric Association, 1994; Mrazek & Haggerty, 1994). In contrast, resilient adolescents have been shown to have support and supervision from a caring adult (Rutter, 1979; Werner & Smith,1992). It seems logical to posit that these two common denominators among youth developing maladaptive outcomes are linked. That is, it is not difficult to imagine the importance of the presence of a caring adult in helping build a youth's self-esteem.

The belief that an adult plays a critical role in the development of a youth's self-esteem is the basic premise upon which mentoring is founded. Mentoring programs attempt to provide youth who lack a caring adult in their lives with an adult "surrogate" in the hopes that this will help improve the youth's self-esteem and ultimately their resiliency in navigating the hazards of adolescence.

> *"The purpose of this chapter is to demonstrate how Harter's (1993) model of self-esteem can help conceptualize the mentoring process. Using this model we show how it can guide mentoring organizations in the planning, implementation, monitoring, and evaluation of their programs."*

The mentoring movement is growing exponentially as evidenced by the President's Summit for America's future in April 1997, America's Promise: The Alliance for Youth. America's Promise was developed to ensure that America's youth have access to five fundamental resources, the first being access to a caring adult. While mentoring organizations recognize that an adult is important in building self-esteem, many have not conceptualized how this process might occur. The importance of understanding the process of how resiliency occurs has been emphasized by many researchers (Coie, 1996; Dishion, Andrews,

Kavanagh, & Soberman, 1996; Kazdin, 1997; Rutter, 1990). In the context of mentoring, the challenge is to understand the process by which an adult mentor interacts with a youth to build self-esteem.

Harter's Model of Self-Esteem as a Useful Model for Mentoring

The purpose of this chapter is to demonstrate how Harter's (1993) model of self-esteem can help conceptualize the mentoring process. Using this model we show how it can guide mentoring organizations in the planning, implementation, monitoring, and evaluation of their programs.

One theory of self-esteem that has received strong empirical support is that of Harter (1993). This theory (founded on the work of James, 1892, and Cooley, 1902) defines global self-esteem as an overall sense of self-worth. Global self-esteem is influenced by two factors, perceived competence in various domains (i.e., areas of one's life), and by the approval one receives from significant others.

"Mentoring programs attempt to provide youth who lack a caring adult in their lives with an adult 'surrogate' in the hopes that this will help improve the youth's self-esteem and ultimately their resiliency in navigating the hazards of adolescence."

With respect to the first factor, the number of domains in which an individual can provide judgments of adequacy and competence is dependent on developmental maturity. Harter (1985) discovered that children can only meaningfully differentiate five domains: scholastic competence, social acceptance, athletic competence, physical appearance, and behavioral conduct. In later research, Harter (1988) found that adolescents can meaningfully provide ratings of competency and adequacy in three additional domains: job competence, romantic appeal, and close friendships.

Harter (1993) adds that it is the discrepancy between competency and perceived importance that affects global self-esteem. Put simply, if children or adolescents perceive they are competent in a domain of value to them, and they obtain approval related to that domain from significant others, it will positively affect global self-esteem. Global self-esteem is affected negatively when an adolescent perceives a domain to be of importance, values approval from significant others in that domain, but lacks competence. Finally, the model has shown that global self-esteem remains relatively unaffected by feelings of incompetence in a particular domain if the adolescent places little value on that domain and/or perceives that it is of little value to significant others.

Hamilton and Darling (1996) define a mentor as: [someone who is] "...an unrelated adult....willing to act as a guide in a new or unfamiliar situation" (p.199). The difficulty with this definition is that it does not specifically address how the mentor is to act or guide; it does not address the issue of process.

Taking Harter's model into consideration we offer the following expanded definition of a mentor:

The mentor is the resiliency catalyst responsible for ensuring that the process of building global self-esteem is realized. This process includes providing opportunities for developing competencies in domains of perceived value and providing the approval for successes and support for failures in developing these competencies.

Application of the Model to the Elements of Successful Mentoring Programs

The National Mentoring Working Group (1996) has published 10 elements necessary for a mentoring program to be effective. These quality assurance standards include: 1) a statement of purpose and long range plan, 2) a recruitment plan for mentors and participants, 3) an orientation for mentors and participants, 4) eligibility screening for mentors and participants, 5) a training curriculum for mentors and participants, 6) a matching strategy, 7) a monitoring process, 8) a support, recognition, and retention process, 9) closure steps, and 10) an evaluation. Harter's model can be applied to many of these standards.

> *"The number one problem facing mentoring organizations is that the demand for mentors outweighs the supply. Recruitment strategies are of paramount importance if America's Promise is to reach its goal of connecting two million young people to a caring adult."*

Recruitment

The number one problem facing mentoring organizations is that the demand for mentors outweighs the supply. Recruitment strategies are of paramount importance if America's Promise is to reach its goal of connecting two million young people to a caring adult. Using the model, recruitment strategies could emphasize that mentors need not fit a particular mold and could be focused on targeting individuals who are competent in each of Harter's domains. Recruitment messages could appeal to mentors by emphasizing the relationship between high self-esteem and well-adjusted adolescents. Such messages could show how a mentor can impact an adolescent's future by simply sharing their unique skills and providing approval.

Orientation

Perhaps even more important than establishing a relationship between a mentor and a child is to ensure that the relationship is enduring. Mentoring organizations must take steps to decrease the likelihood of exposing vulnerable youth to another failed relationship. One approach to meeting this goal is to provide individuals interested in entering a mentoring relationship with realistic expectations of what such a relationship involves. Both parties must realize that building trust, identifying areas of mutual interest, and the *process* of developing competencies require an extended time commitment.

Screening & Matching

A key goal of mentoring organizations is to match mentors to protégés with similar interests. This is often done intuitively by a caseworker who screens both parties. Harter's model could

> *"Both parties must realize that building trust, identifying areas of mutual interest, and the process of developing competencies require an extended time commitment."*

provide mentoring organizations with another source of rationale on which to base their matching strategy. For example, during their initial screening, case workers could gather information on the needs, interests, and competencies of both mentor and protégé using Harter's self-perception profiles (1985,1986, 1988).

Some form of profile matching using the domains identified by Harter (1985, 1988) and Neeman and Harter (1986) might prove useful in matching mentors with protégés. The profile matching might prove a useful tool in helping to flag potential problems in matching. For example, in instances where the results of the profile matching and the intuition of the case-worker are in agreement, the mentoring organization can have more confidence that the match will be successful. However, in cases where the results of the profiles are at odds with those of the caseworker it may serve as a signal that the feasibility of the match should be reexamined.

Training

A goal of mentoring organizations must be to provide mentors with the skills they need to be a complete mentor. It is very difficult to obtain the perfect match. Undoubtedly, the protégé will request that the mentor provide support and guidance in a domain in which the mentor lacks such skills. Programs must be able to provide mentors interested in acquiring new skills with the resources to do so. But where to begin? The model could be used to identify the basic areas around which training manuals and seminars could be developed, namely in the domains identified by Harter's research including academics, athletics, job competence, behavioral conduct, and the development and maintenance of interpersonal relationships.

> *"The model could be used to identify the basic areas around which training manuals and seminars could be developed, namely in the domains identified by Harter's research including academics, athletics, job competence, behavioral conduct, and the development and maintenance of interpersonal relationships."*

Monitoring

Another goal of the mentoring program must be to include an ongoing assessment of the quality of the mentor-protégé relationship. What structure should this monitoring take? Using the model as a guide, caseworkers could monitor whether both mentor and protégé are indeed spending time developing competency in activities valued by both. The mentor and adolescent must also regard each other as important or the mentoring program will fail (Daloz, 1986; Erkut & Mokros,

1984; Torrance, 1983). This is consistent with Cooley's (1902) and Harter's (1993) emphasis on the importance of approval from significant others. If both parties agree to their mutual importance, it is necessary to establish whether the communication between mentor and adolescent is effective. Kalbfleisch and Davies (1993), for example, assessed the communication competence, perceived risk in intimacy, and self-esteem in mentor-protégé relationships. Such indices are critical in establishing the quality of a mentoring relationship and are often included as process outcomes in evaluations.

Evaluation

Very few intervention programs aimed at improving self-esteem have undergone a scientifically based evaluation. Some notable exceptions include Seligman's Penn State Program (Seligman, 1995), the Outward Bound Program (Hattie & Marsh, 1996), and Big Brothers/Big Sisters (Tierney, Grossman, & Resch, 1995). [See chapters one, two, and four for more information on the BB/BS evaluation.] For the most part, however, mentoring programs have not included an evaluation component and, consequently, they have failed to demonstrate their effectiveness, causing some to question their utility (Kellerman, Fuqua-Whitley, & Rivara, 1996).

Theory forms the foundation of program evaluation. Without such a foundation, program planners and evaluators cannot be sure what is working, what should be changed, and why. Evaluation should consider both short-term and long-term outcomes. Using the model as a guide, short-term outcomes might include change in competency in valued domains, time spent on those domains, and changes in self-esteem. Other short-term outcomes might include a reduction in the symptoms associated with various behavioral and emotional problems. Long-term outcomes might include reduction in the incidence in diagnosed cases of behavioral and emotional problems in which a lack of adult support and guidance and low self-esteem are common denominators. As noted in the introduction these include depression, eating disorders, academic failure, delinquent behavior, and substance abuse.

> *"For the most part ... mentoring programs have not included an evaluation component and, consequently, they have failed to demonstrate their effectiveness, causing some to question their utility. Theory forms the foundation of program evaluation. Without such a foundation, program planners and evaluators cannot be sure what is working."*

Summary: Harter's Model as a Job Description
for Mentoring Organizations

According to Harter's (1993) model, global self-esteem arises from perceptions of being competent in valued domains of one's life and from the approval of significant others. Unfortunately, vulnerable adolescents often lack an adult who perceives similar domains to be of value, who possesses the skills necessary to help the adolescent achieve competency in these domains, and who can provide the approval they require to build self-esteem. In such cases, a mentor can act as a resiliency catalyst, guiding the adolescent through the process of building self-esteem.

The need for a theory to guide the mentoring process can be likened to the need for a job description. A thorough understanding of what the job entails is required to recruit, screen, orient, train, monitor, and evaluate the success of applicants. Harter's model provides such a job description for mentoring organizations to achieve these same goals.

> "The need for a theory to guide the mentoring process can be likened to the need for a job description."

The relationship of self-esteem to various youth problems and psychopathologies raises the possibility that one program may help prevent or reduce a variety of problems. Such an approach has intuitive appeal in terms of cost effectiveness. More importantly, there is some evidence that such "general" approaches work (e.g., Allen, Phillibei, Herrling, & Kupermic, 1997), perhaps better than those aimed at the specific symptoms of a particular disorder (Smolak, in press). Indeed, prevention specialists have argued that disorder specific approaches are not likely to be successful (Albee, 1987). In light of these arguments, mentoring has great potential as a general approach to prevention, serving to improve self-esteem and subsequently resiliency toward a variety of maladaptive outcomes. ➤

References

Albee, G. (1987). The rationale and need for primary prevention. In S. Goldston (Ed.), *Concepts of primary prevention: A framework for program development* (pp. 7-20). Sacramento, CA: California Dept of Mental Health.

Allen, J., Philliber, S., Herrling, S., & Kuperminc, G. (1997). Preventing teen pregnancy and academic failure: Experimental evaluation of a developmentally based approach. *Child Development, 64,* 729-742.

American Psychiatric Association. Diagnostic and statistical manual of mental disorders (4th Ed.), (1994). Washington, DC.

Button, E.J., Sonuga-Barke, E.J.S., Davies, J., & Thompson, M. (1996). A prospective study of self-esteem in the prediction of eating problems in adolescent schoolgirls: Questionnaire findings. *British Journal of Clinical Psychology, 35,* 193-203.

Coie, J.D. (1996). Prevention of violence and antisocial behavior. In R.D. Peters & R.J. McMahon (Eds.), *Preventing childhood disorders, substance abuse and delinquency* (pp. 1-18). California: Sage Publications.

Cooley, C. H. (1902). *Human nature and the social order.* New York, NY: Scribner's.

Daloz, L.A. (1986). *Effective teaching and mentoring: Realizing the transformational power of adult learning experiences.* San Francisco, CA: Jossey-Bass.

Dishion, T.J., Andrews, D.W., Kavanagh, K., & Soberman, L.H. (1996). Preventive interventions for high-risk youth: The adolescent transition program. In R.D. Peters & R.J. McMahon (Eds.), *Preventing childhood disorders, substance abuse and delinquency* (pp. 184-214). Newbury Park, CA: Sage Publications.

Dubois, D.L., Felner, R.D., Sherman, M.D., & Bull, C.A. (1994). Socioenvironmental experiences, self-esteem, and emotional/behavioral problem in early adolescence. *American Journal of Community Psychology, 22* (3), 371-397.

Erkut, S., & Mokros, J.R. (1984). Professors as models and mentors for college students. *American Educational Research Journal, 21*, 399-417.

Hamilton, S. F., & Darling, N. (1996). Mentors in adolescents' lives. In K. Hurrelmann & S.F. Hamilton (Eds.), *Social problems and social contexts in adolescence: Perspectives across boundaries* (pp. 199-215). New York, NY: Aldine de Gruyter.

Harter, S. (1985). *Manual for the Self-Perception Profile for Children*. Denver, CO: University of Denver.

Harter, S. (1988). *Manual for the Self-Perception Profile for Adolescents*. Denver, CO: University of Denver.

Harter, S. (1993). Causes and consequences of low self-esteem in children and adolescents. In R.F. Baumeister (Ed.). *Self-esteem: The puzzle of low self-regard* (pp. 87-116). New York, NY: Plenum Press.

Hattie, J., & Marsh, H.W. (1996). Future directions in self-concept research. In B.A. Bracken (Ed.), *Handbook of self-concept: Developmental, social, and clinical considerations* (pp. 421-462). New York, NY: John Wiley & Sons.

James, W. (1890). *Principles of Psychology*. Chicago, IL: Encyclopedia Britannica.

Jessor, R. (1993). Successful adolescent development among youth in high-risk settings. *American Psychologist, 48*, 117-126.

Kalbfleisch, P.J., & Davies, A.B. (1993). An interpersonal model for participation in mentoring relationships. *Western Journal of Communication*, 399-415.

Kazdin, A.E. (1997). Conduct disorder across the life-span. In S.S. Luthar, J.A. Burack, D. Ciccchetti, & J.R. Weisz (Eds.), *Developmental psychopathology* (pp. 248-272). New York, NY: Cambridge University Press.

Kellerman, A.L., Fuqua-Whitley, D.S., & Rivara, F.P. (1996). *Preventing youth violence: A summary of program evaluations*. Report from America's Promise, Seattle, WA: University of Washington.

Keith, L. K., & Bracken, B.A. (1996). Self-concept instrumentation: A historical and evaluative review. In B.A. Bracken (Ed.), *Handbook of self-concept: Developmental, social, and clinical considerations* (pp. 91-170). New York, NY: John Wiley & Sons.

Marton, P., Connolly, J., Kutcher, S., & Korenblum, M. (1993).Cognitive social skills and social self-appraisal in depressed adolescents. *Journal of the American Academy of Child and Adolescent Psychiatry, 32*, 739-744.

Mrazek, P.J. & Haggerty, R.J. (Eds.). (1994). *Reducing risks for mental disorders: Frontiers for preventive intervention research*. Washington, D.C.: National Academy Press.

National Mentoring Working Group (1996). *Mentoring: Elements of effective practice*. Washington, DC.

Neemann, J., & Harter, S. (1986). *Manual for the self-perception profile for college students*. Denver, CO: University of Denver.

Roberts, A., & Cotton, L. (1994). Note on assessing a mentor program. *Psychological Reports, 75*, 1369-1370.

Rutter, M. (1979). Protective factors in children's responses to stress and disadvantage. In M.W. Kent & J.E. Rolf (Eds.), *Primary prevention in psychopathology. Vol. 3: Social competence in children* (pp.49-74). Hanover, NH: University Press of New England.

Rutter, M. (1990). Psychosocial resilience and protective mechanisms. In J. Rolf, A.S. Masten, D. Cicchetti, K.H. Neuchterlein, & S. Weintraub (Eds.), *Risk and protective factors in the development of psychopathology* (pp. 181-214). New York, NY: Cambridge University Press.

Seligman, M. (1995). *The optimistic child*. Boston, MA: Houghton Mifflin Company.

Shisslak, C.M., Crago, M., Estes, L.S., & Gray, N. (1996). Content and method of developmentally appropriate prevention programs. In L. Smolak, M. Levine, & R. Striegel-Moore (Eds.), *The developmental psychopathology of eating disorders* (pp. 341- 363). Mahwah, NJ: Lawrence Erlbaum.

Smolak, L. (in press). Suggestions for the content and structure of elementary school curricula for the primary prevention of eating problems. In Piran, N., Levine, M.P., & Steiner-Adair, C. (in press). *Preventing eating disorders: A handbook of interventions and special challenges*. Philadelphia, PA: Brunner/Mazel.

Tierney, J.P., Grossman, J.B., & Resch, N.L. (1995). *Making a difference: An impact study of Big Brothers/Big Sisters*. Philadelphia, PA: Public/Private Ventures.

Taylor, J.L., Gilligan, C., & Sullivan, A.M. (1995). *Between voices and silence*. Cambridge, MA: Harvard University Press.

Torrance, E.P. (1983). Role of mentors in creative achievement. *Creative Child and Adult Quarterly, 3,* 8-15.

Turner, S., Norman, E., & Zunz, S. (1995). Enhancing resiliency in girls and boys: A case for gender specific adolescent programming. *The Journal of Primary Prevention, 16* (1), 25-38.

Werner, E., & Smith, R. (1992).*Overcoming the odds: High risk children from birth to adulthood.* Ithaca, NY: Cornell University Press.

Ralph Renger, Ph.D., is an Assistant Professor in the Arizona Prevention Center at the University of Arizona. He is working closely with the local alliance of mentoring organizations to improve the quality and quantity of mentoring relationships. He can be reached by phone (520-882-5852, ext. 17) or by e-mail (renger@u.arizona.edu).

Pamela J. Kalbfleisch, Ph.D., is an Associate Professor in the Department of Communication and Mass Media at the University of Wyoming in Laramie, Wyoming. She can be reached by phone (307-766-3857) or by e-mail (pamelak@uwyo.edu).

Marjorie Crago, Ph.D., is a Research Specialist at the University of Arizona Prevention Center in Tucson. She can be reached by e-mail (crago@u.arizona.edu).

Linda Smolak, Ph.D., is Professor of Psychology at Kenyan College, Gambier, OH. She can be reached by phone (740-427-5374) or by e-mail (smolak@kenyon.edu).

Acknowledgments

The authors would like to thank Dr. Susan Harter, Dr. Harry McDermott, Sgt. Robert Holliday, and Ms. Susan French Fry for their contributions to this manuscript.

Jason Thomas: Returning to the Inner City to "Make a Difference for Kids"

by Nan Henderson, M.S.W.

Jason Thomas' story illustrates the power of an environment filled with strands of the Resiliency Wheel (see Figure 1 in Preface)—i.e., pro-social bonding, clear and consistent boundaries, life skills taught and modeled, caring and support, high expectations for success, and opportunities for meaningful participation. In addition, his life shows how "adaptive distancing" in the form of the non-personalization of racial bigotry can provide a means of personal coping with such injustice, and it shows the power of both having and being a mentor. Acutely aware of how many children don't have the environmental support he was "blessed with" growing up in the inner city of Dayton, Ohio, he has returned to his community to provide to others some of what made the difference for him.

Jason Thomas is the first to admit that he beat the odds. "I'm a kid from the inner city, and no one would expect that; people that have met me outside of the area I've grown up in think I've grown up in some suburb or some area of town that has a lot of money, and that's not the case."

A business graduate of Texas Southern University, 28-year-old Jason now works as a student assistance provider at the elementary and high school levels in Dayton, Ohio public schools. Many of his childhood friends, however, have experienced different life outcomes. "My closest friend got killed because he was strung out on drugs; he walked in front of a car," Jason said.

> "*I'm a kid from the inner city, and no one would expect that; people that have met me outside of the area I've grown up in think I've grown up in some suburb or some area of town that has a lot of money, and that's not the case.*"

"[Over the years,] my mother would always call me and say, 'You know such-and-such got shot. You know that one kid you used to hang with? He's dead,' or 'such-and-such is in jail.' It was sad because these are the same kids that had the same potential that I had but they chose a different direction in life than I chose."

What made the difference for Jason? He credits his mother and his father, neither of whom went to college, but both of whom had high expectations for him. His mother managed the apartments where Jason and his family lived and his father was the head maintenance person there. "My dad always used to stress to me to live at least twice as good as he's ever lived because his father wasn't around when he was younger. He made a lot of sacrifices in order [for me] to have things that he didn't have when he was growing up."

He also credits a lot of people in his life, "so many different people who have helped me throughout the years," his involvement in sports, and a tragedy that hit his family when Jason was only five. That year, his only sibling, a sister about two years older than he, died from sickle cell anemia. "Adversity was in our household when I was very young," he said. "Dealing with that was tough because something and somebody wasn't there anymore. I was thinking about her actually this morning," Jason added. "We would do a lot of playing and she [would] keep me active, trying to keep me out of trouble because she was my big sister.

"I use that for inner strength when times have gotten hard; I've [said to] myself, 'That could have been me.' The chance of me having the sickle cell trait since she had it was like 50%. So I figure God has put me here for a reason, and hopefully I'm carrying out his mission somehow. But it was tough."

"My Mom is One of the Strongest People on Earth"

"I think my mom was probably the strongest one because she had to bear the burden of having a child and then losing something so precious. I think my mom is one of the strongest people on this earth," Jason observed. "She's really dealt with a lot in her life time, and I feed off of that. I look at her and [think], man, my mother is tough."

She was also tough on Jason. "[My family] was pretty close knit," Jason said. "They were very open and made me feel [that] I wouldn't have to hide anything from them like

> *"'I think my mom is one of the strongest people on this earth,' Jason observed. 'She's really dealt with a lot in her life time, and I feed off of that. I look at her and [think], man, my mother is tough.'"*

doing bad in school. Nine times out of 10 I wouldn't even have a chance to [do poorly] because my mother was so on top of things. She knew [if I'd had a bad] week of school because she was always communicating with my teachers and the administrator at the school just to make sure I was on top of my Ps and Qs, as she would say. My mother and my father would never let me slip. I was blessed to have two wonderful parents; it was important for them to push me as far as they could academically."

Jason added that for many years he didn't push himself to the degree that his parents wanted. A main reason, he explained, was "I felt uncomfortable doing much better than my classmates. I just wanted to fit in at the time; then after I realized how important it was in my junior and senior year, I really started to push myself because I was trying to earn a basketball scholarship."

Sports helped him "in a tremendous way," Jason said, and sports also helped others he knew. His parents introduced him to organized sports when he was in fourth grade. "Sports," he said, "helped me avoid a lot of the obstacles that are out there for some of the youth that don't have organized activities, so their minds are wandering, and there's a lot of idle time. Sports also exposed me to different cultures, to ethnic differences at a young age." Being involved in sports also gave him and others "a sense of focus and direction,

> **"My mother and my father would never let me slip. I was blessed to have two wonderful parents; it was important for them to push me as far as they could academically."**

and it tugged the academics along with it because we knew we couldn't do one without the other."

Jason's mother was always looking for other ways to help her son academically. When he was in seventh grade, she found the man Jason still calls, "my mentor, Richard Gates. He started tutoring me; he took me under his wing," Jason recalled. "He was somebody I could relate to because we have a lot in common as far as the way he grew up. He also went to college on a basketball scholarship." Jason continued, "Some of the things he said had a big influence on me. He would ask me questions [like], 'What do you plan on being 10 years from now?' We also did other things other than him just tutoring me. I participated in some of his programs and some of his summer basketball games, so we kept in really close contact. He was almost like a second father to me."

> **"Being involved in sports also gave him and others 'a sense of focus and direction, and it tugged the academics along with it because we knew we couldn't do one without the other.'"**

Mr. Gates is now Dr. Gates, Jason said, and has helped countless students like himself both academically and in his athletic programs. "He's always helped someone try to succeed in life. He did this for free. My mother found him through word of mouth. She was looking for a tutor and a friend of hers told her about him and that's how we became really close."

Dealing with Racism

In her quest "to further my education," Jason's mother enrolled him in parochial school when he was in the sixth grade. Even then, Jason was the star basketball player, and for the first time the school won the Catholic Youth Organization championship. To celebrate, Jason stayed over night at a friend's house who also attended his school, and the next day, he encountered blatant racism for the first time.

"We were playing outside and one of [my friend's] friends called me a nigger. I had heard other people talk about it, you know, but this was my first time," Jason said. "I was boiling inside. I didn't know how to react [other than] go chasing him. He ran, naturally, and nothing happened other than I called my father and said, 'Come and get me.' I just felt uncomfortable."

Jason added: "It made me wonder who else in this school thinks that I'm not Jason, I'm just some nigger going to this school?" Though there was one other African American in his class, Jason said, "There was probably no one else [in the school] that had come from the inner city, from the same background that I'd come from. So it was a difficult time for me, it was in the middle of the year, so that meant I had another half the year before I could finish up." He added, "There was this bitter anger in me that I didn't know how to let out. I was happy to get that year over with." Jason said he ran into the same group of guys when he was a senior in high school. "We were playing their school, a Catholic high school here in the city. And there was a totally different reaction [from them]. It was more a 'hey, I know him; he's a friend of mine.' I think they had grown, had learned that wherever they had learned that term or that behavior, it wasn't going to wash in life. [That second encounter] was good for both of us."

> *"It made me wonder who else in this school thinks that I'm not Jason, I'm just some nigger going to this school?"*

Another incidence of the racism Jason has encountered in his life occurred when he was beginning his senior year in college in Houston, Texas. He had just broken his ankle in a basketball game, and while he was driving home to his apartment, he was trying to come to terms with the reality that he wouldn't play his senior year. "Two young men, who happened to be white, drove along next to me and yelled racial slurs. Then these two tried to run me off the highway," Jason said. The incident caught him off guard because he'd not experienced anything like it previously in the three years he'd been in Texas. "These kids had just graduated from high school, they were drunk. And an off-duty policeman, who happened to be Hispanic, saw the whole thing and followed us. It seemed like God was watching me because it could have turned into a big catastrophe. They had run into my car, and it turned into a big mess; he took a report and arrested them."

When asked how he has come to terms with these kinds of experiences, Jason again credited his mother. She gave him a history lesson, he said, that gave him a perspective. "She started with how the slave trade evolved, she just broke it down as to different things that happened in history which caused the predicament society is in now. It pretty much came down to greed. She made me understand that we have these racial hang-ups due to greed and economic development. It's really not a black and white issue."

"You Have to Beat People with Your Mind Instead of Your Hands"

"Racial issues were never emphasized in my house," Jason continued. He said the message was, "Those things are going to be there, and you have to be a strong enough person to deal with it when it happens. My mother would always say, 'You can't beat the whole world up, and beating one person up isn't going to solve the problems of today. So you might as well give that up.' After I cried in my room a few times about different things that happened racially, it made me more aware of what she was saying...it was more or less that you have to beat people with your mind instead of with your hands."

> *"My Mother would always say, 'You can't beat the whole world up, and beating one person up isn't going to solve the problems of today. So you might as well give that up.'"*

Jason said that when he was growing up he also developed a close friendship with another basketball player, Ron Harper, who now plays for the Chicago Bulls. Ron became a role model to Jason; "he's like a godbrother to me." Jason explained, "When I didn't want to call my mother or my father, or I didn't want to talk to Mr. Gates, I could always call Ron because he was only five years older and I was always around him as a kid. I looked up to him because he was a good athlete." Ron overcame a lot, too, Jason added. "People would talk about him and say he was ignorant and dumb due to the fact he has this speech impediment. Growing up I saw that when the odds were against him, he went against the odds and showed everybody that what they were saying was wrong.

"Ron was a big influence in my life," Jason said. "Mr. Gates was the one that actually [brought] us together." His decision to return to Dayton after his graduation from college was largely based on a desire to provide for kids what Mr. Gates and Ron Harper provided for him. "I didn't want to be a statistic in the sense of another kid from the city goes off to college, and doesn't come home with his degree, doesn't do anything to help his community," Jason explained. So he did come home, despite the racial barriers that still exist in his community.

"Dayton is a city that is still divided, racially," Jason said. "East side is predominantly white; west side is still predominantly black. It's one of these traditional towns, set in its ways...the type of town where opportunities are going to be limited to a degree because there are people on this side of town who look at you as, 'there's that nigger.' Then there are people on your own side of town that don't want to see you succeed. They're jealous of the fact that you did get an education, you did do well in sports, you did do something positive with your life. And [they] don't want to see you do any more. So, you have to deal with that."

"I let [students] know that someone here does care, even if they are not getting that attention at home."

Jason said, however, that he felt that he "could make a difference in my neighborhood and in the community because I was a well-liked person as far as the older generation and the younger generation. I felt I could be a positive influence on these kids. A lot of their parents were in high school watching me play basketball growing up." It is easier for kids to relate to someone who is good at something they are interested in, Jason explained. "It's like how Mr. Gates got me."

Giving Kids the Support that Many Don't Get at Home

He said his work with students is especially gratifying because it enables him to "hit a broad base, not just the kids on the west side, but also the kids on the east side, the north side, and the south side." In working with kids, he recalls all the things his parents did for him, including "the music and the sports so I wouldn't have that idle time to do negative things out on the street," as well as the fact that everyone knew when he was growing up, "I had to be in when the street lights came on, or else my father would be hollering out the window." Many

> *"I didn't want to be a statistic in the sense of another kid from the city goes off to college, and doesn't come home with his degree, doesn't do anything to help his community."*

kids today, he added, don't have that support at home, so "I'm able to give it to them in school. That's what I really enjoy, the personal satisfaction when [I] can actually make a difference in kids' lives, [be] someone they look forward to...because I tell you as soon as I get in the [school] building, my door is bombarded with [children knocking], 'Mr. Thomas, Mr. Thomas, can I come in?'"

He said he meets with students in the elementary school who are referred by teachers for improvement in communication skills, social skills, or conflict resolution. "One new item I added this year was time management; I think that is very important for a lot of our young people today...a lot of their time is being spent unconstructively. If they knew how to manage their time properly, they could become better students." In addition to meeting with students in half-hour individual sessions, Jason meets with groups of eight students two or three times a week, and tutors "those kids that are having problems understanding the work before they go home" every day during the last hour of school. "I meet with probably 60 kids a day, " he said.

When they come knocking on his door most of the children are just wanting "conversation, just an open conversation," Jason explained. "I look young, so they can relate to me. A lot of times I just sit down and talk to them and ask them how their weekend was, or give them something positive so they can have a productive day or a productive week. I can see a difference in a lot of them [just from this interaction], because they are starving for attention and they aren't getting it at home. I try to give my time, I try to give them extra support. I'll stop by the class and just say 'hello' to let them know that someone here does care, even if they are not getting that attention at home.

"Sometimes," Jason added, "I give them advice on certain things they are doing that might trigger a reaction from their teacher, something that might help

> *"A lot of times I just sit down and talk to them and ask them how their week-end was, or give them something positive so they can have a productive day or a productive week. I can see a difference in a lot of them [just from this interaction], because they are starving for attention and they aren't getting it at home."*

them become better students so that they don't run into the same problems all of the time. They usually listen and say, 'O.K. Thanks, Mr. Thomas.' Later I will ask, 'Did you tell your teacher good morning, or did you tell your teacher goodbye?' Basic little social skills to see if they can get a different reaction. As far as conflict resolution, I'll ask, 'Do you ever speak to your friends in a positive way instead of demeaning and tearing them down and talking about them?' And they try those things and they see a difference...It makes them better people, it makes them...more resilient.

"And that makes me feel good inside, just to be a little help. I love my job."

Nan Henderson, M.S.W., is a national speaker and consultant on fostering resiliency and wellness, alcohol and other drug issues, and on organizational change. She has coauthored/edited five books about resiliency, and is the Editor-in-chief at Resiliency In Action, Inc. She can be reached at Nan Henderson and Associates, 5130 La Jolla Blvd., #2K, San Diego, CA 92109, p/f (858-488-5034), or by e-mail: (nanh@connectnet.com).

How to Be a Turnaround Teacher/Mentor

by Bonnie Benard, M.S.W.

Reprinted with permission from Reaching Today's Youth, *Spring 1998.*

Can you identify a special teacher or mentor in your life? What was it about him or her that influenced you? This chapter provides a set of best practices for working with "high-risk" young people derived from the approaches and strategies that have been used successfully by "turnaround teachers" for generations.

> *One of the most wonderful things we see now in adulthood is that these children really remember one or two teachers who made the difference. They mourn some of those teachers more than they do their own family members because what went out of their lives was a person who looked beyond outward experience, their behavior, and their oftentimes unkempt appearance, and saw the promise.*
>
> —*Emmy Werner (1996, pp. 24-25)*

For over a decade public and educational discourse has been steeped in the language of risk. Between 1989 and 1994 alone, more than 2,500 articles were published on "children and families at risk" (Swadner & Lubeck, 1995, p. 1). Over 40 years of social science research has clearly identified poverty—the direct result of public abdication of responsibility for human welfare—as the factor most likely to put a person "at risk" for social ills such as drug abuse, teen pregnancy, child abuse, violence, and school failure.

Yet policymakers, politicians, the media, and often researchers themselves have personalized "at-riskness" by locating it in youth, their families, and cultures—perhaps providing a convenient smokescreen for the naming and blaming of poverty. Even when its use is well intentioned (e.g., when used to secure needed services for children and families), this approach has increasingly led to harmful, isolating practices for a growing number of students in urban schools.

Most dangerous of all, this risk focus has encouraged teachers and other helping professionals to see children and families only through a deficit lens. This "glass-as-half-empty" perspective blocks our vision to see the whole person and hear the "real story"—often one filled with strengths and capacity. Wehmiller (1992) warns,

> When we don't know each other's stories, we substitute our own myth about who that person is. When we are operating with only a myth, none of that person's truth will ever be known to us, and we will injure them—mostly without ever meaning to (p. 380).

Resilience: An Alternative Way of Seeing

Indeed, this "mythical" lens *is* injurious, quickly translating into a racist, classist, sexist, or ageist perspective. While our common sense alone cautions us against such an approach, there is an even more concrete reason to reject it. We now have the most rigorous scientific research on human development—prospective longitudinal studies—that should put our preoccupation with risk to rest permanently. These studies on how individuals develop successfully despite risk and adversity certainly prove the lack of predictive power of risk factors. Researchers worldwide have documented the amazing finding that, when tracked into adulthood, at least 50%, and usually close to 70%, of "high-risk" children grow up to be not only successful by societal indicators but also "confident, competent, and caring" persons (Werner & Smith, 1992).

The personal attitudes and competencies most often associated with these resilient individuals include the broad categories of social competence, metacognition, autonomy, and a sense of purpose and belief in a bright future. While many researchers and practitioners have latched onto these personal attributes, creating a myriad of social—and life—skills programs to teach them directly, the strong message of resilience research is that these attributes are expressions—not causes— of resilience. Werner and Smith (1992) refer to resilience as an innate "self-righting mechanism" (p. 202) and Lifton (1994) identifies resilience as the human capacity of *all* individuals to transform and change—no matter their risks. Human beings are genetically hard-wired to form relationships (social competence), to problem solve (metacognition), to develop a sense of identity (autonomy), and to plan and hope (a sense of purpose and future). These are the growth capacities which have enabled survival throughout human history.

However, even though some individuals can express these capacities in the absence of a facilitative environment, it is clearly the presence of a *nurturing* climate that draws them forth and encourages their expression. This finding is perhaps the most important and prescriptive for educators and other mentors. The research shows that, contrary to much popular belief, teachers and schools actually do have the power to tip the scales from risk to resilience.

Werner and Smith (1989) found that "among the most frequently encountered positive role models for children, outside their circle of family members, was a favorite teacher. For the resilient youngster, a special teacher was not just an instructor for academic skills, but also a confident and positive model for personal identification" (p. 162). Repeatedly, these turnaround teachers and mentors are described as building, in their own personal styles and ways, three crucial environmental protective factors: connection, competence, and contribution.

Turnaround Teachers and Mentors Provide *Connection*

Turnaround teachers/mentors are characterized, first and foremost, as caring individuals who develop relationships with their students. They convey the message that they are " there for" a youth through trust and unconditional love. To the greatest extent possible, they help meet the basic survival need of overwhelmed students and their families. On a more comprehensive level, they may connect students and their families to outside community resources in order to find food, shelter, clothing, counseling, treatment, and additional mentoring.

Providing connection also translates into meeting emotional safety needs. Resilient survivors talk about teachers' "quiet availability," "fundamental positive regard," and "simple sustained kindness," such

> **Believeing in our students' resilience requires foremost that we believe in our own innate capacity to transform and change.**

as a touch on the shoulder, a smile, or a greeting (Higgins, 1994, pp. 324-25). Being interested in, actively listening to, and validating the feelings of struggling young people, as well as getting to know their strengths and gifts, conveys the message, "You matter." According to renowned urban educator Deborah Meier (1995), this kind of respect—having a person "acknowledge us, see us for who we are, as their equal in value and importance" (p. 120)—figures high in turnaround relationships.

Finally, these individuals connect with their students by showing compassion—nonjudgemental support that looks beneath the students' negative behavior and sees their pain and suffering. They do not take students' behavior personally, no matter how negative it may be, but understand instead that the student is doing the best he or she can, given his or her experiences. Sandy McBrayer, founder of an alternative school for homeless youth and 1994 National Teacher of the Year, declares, "People ask me what my 'methods' are. I don't have a method. But I believe one of the things that makes me an adequate or proficient teacher is that I never judge... and I tell my kids I love them every day" (Bacon, 1995, p. 44). This rapport is also the critical motivational foundation for successful learning. As Noddings points out, "It is obvious that children will work harder and do things—even odd things like adding fractions—for people they love and trust" (p. 32).

Turnaround Teachers and Mentors Build *Competence*

At the core of caring relationships are positive and high expectations that not only structure and guide behavior, but also challenge students to perform beyond what they believe they can do. These expectations reflect a deep belief in the student's innate competence and self-righting capacities. A consistent description of turnaround teachers/mentors is that they see the possibility: "They held visions of us that we could not imagine for ourselves" (Delpit, 1996, p. 199).

However, turnaround teachers/mentors not only see the possibilities, they also recognize existing competencies and mirror them back, helping students appreciate where they are already strong. When they use these strengths, interests, goals, and dreams as the beginning point for learning, they tap the student's intrinsic motivation and existing, innate drive for learning. Positive and high expectations then become easier for students to meet.

This identification of strengths can especially assist overwhelmed, labeled, and oppressed youth in reframimng their narratives from "damaged victims" to "resilient survivors." Turnaround teachers/mentors help youth to avoid:

- Taking *personally* the adversity in their lives ("You aren't the cause—nor can you control— your father's drinking");
- Seeing adversity as *permanent* ("This too shall pass"; "Your future will be different"); and
- Seeing setbacks as *pervasive* ("You can rise above this"; "This is only one part of your life experience") (adapted from Seligman, 1995).

Instead, they build their students' sense of competency by teaching metacognition—the understanding of how thoughts influence feelings and behaviors. When students recognize their own conditioned thinking—the environmental messages they have internalized that they are not good enough, smart enough, thin enough, and so on—they can remove blocks to their innate resilience, For example, in a Miami, Florida study, the dropout rate for youth from a public housing community fell to nearly zero when they were taught they had this power to construct the meaning they gave everything that happened to them (Mills, 1991).

Turnaround Teachers and Mentors Let Young People *Contribute*

Rutter and his colleagues (1979), in their seminal research on effective urban schools in poor communities—schools in which the rates of delinquency and dropping out actually declined the longer students were in them—found a striking similarity among them. All of the schools gave students "a lot of responsibility. [Students] participated very actively in all sorts of things that went on in the school: they were treated as responsible people and they reacted accordingly" (1984, p. 65).

Indeed, providing outlets for student contribution is a natural outgrowth of working from this strengths-based perspective. In a physically and psychologically safe and structured environment, opportunities for participation can include:

- Asking questions that encourage self-reflection, critical thinking, and dialogue (especially around salient social and personal issues);
- Making learning more experimental, as in service learning;
- Helping others through community service, peer helping, and cooperative learning;
- Involving students in curriculum planning and giving them choices in their learning experiences;
- Using participatory evaluation strategies; and
- Involving students in creating the governing rules of the classroom.

Even in such classroom discipline issues, student participation can have surprising benefits. "Bring the kids in on it!" Alfie Kohn (1993) urges. "Instead of reaching for coercion, engage children and youth in a conversation about the underlying causes of what is happening and work together to negotiate a solution" (p. 14). When we invite students to help create the classroom rules and school policies, we ensure their buy-in, ownership, and sense of belonging. Perhaps more importantly, we also build their ability to make responsible choices. "It is in the classrooms and families where participation is valued above adult control that students have the chance to learn *self-control*" (Kohn, 1993, p. 18).

The Beliefs of Turnaround Teachers and Mentors

Certain programmatic approaches such as those described in "How To Support Turnaround Teachers" on the following page have proven particularly effective in providing opportunities for active participation and contribution. However, resilience research points out over and over that transformational power exists not in programmatic approaches *per se*, but at the deeper level of relationships, beliefs and expectations, and the willingness to share power. In other words, it is *how* adults do what they do that counts.

Asa Hillard (1991) advises

> to restructure we must first look deeply at the goals that we set for
> our children and the beliefs that we have about them. Once we are
> on the right track there, then we must turn our attention to the
> delivery systems, as we have begun to do. Cooperative learning is
> right. Technology access for all is right. Multiculturalism is right.
> *But none of these approaches or strategies will mean anything if the
> fundamental belief system does not fit the new structures that are
> being created* (p. 36).

The starting point for creating classrooms and schools and programs that tap students' capacities is the deep belief of all staff that every youth is resilient. This means that every adult must personally grapple with questions like "What tapped my resilience? What occurred in my life that brought out my strength and capacity? How am I connecting this knowledge to what I do in the classroom or in this program?"

Believing in students' resilience requires foremost that adults believe in their own innate capacity to transform and change. Our walk always speaks louder than our talk. So to teach students about their internal power, adults must first see that they have the power—no matter what external stresses they face—to let go of conditioned thinking and access innate capacities for compassion, intuition, self-efficacy, and hope. Only when this belief is in place are adults truly able to create the connections, point out the competence, and invite the contribution that will engage the innate resilience in students.

Resiliency Research of Your Own

In the coming weeks or months, try an initial experiment of your own using the resiliency approach. Choose one of your most challenging children or youth. Spend at least a few minutes each day building your connection with that person. Look for and identify all of his or her competencies. Mirror back those strengths. Teach that student that he or she has the power to create his or her own reality. Create opportunities to have the student participate and contribute his or her strengths. Be patient. Focus on small victories—they often grow into major transformations.

But in the meanwhile, relax, have fun, and trust the process! Working from your own innate resilience and well-being engages the same elements in young people. Thus, teaching, facilitating, and leading becomes much more effortless and enjoyable. Resiliency research, as well as studies on nurturing teachers and successful schools, provides the *proof* needed of the benefits of lightening up, letting go of tight control, being patient, and trusting the process.

Finally, know that you are making a difference. When you care, believe in, and "invite back" our most precious resource—our children and youth—you are not only enabling their healthy development and successful learning. You are, indeed, creating inside-out social change, building the compassion and creative citizenry of the future that will restore our lost vision of social and economic justice. ➤

References

Bacon, J. (1995). The place for life and learning: National Teacher of the Year. Sandra McBrayer. *Journal of Emotional and Behavioral Problems. 3*(4), 42-45.

Children's Express (1993). *Voices from the future: Children tell us about violence in America.* New York, NY: Crown.

Delpit, L. (1996). The politics of teaching literate discourse. In W. Ayers & P. Ford (Eds.), *City kids, city teachers: Reports from the front row.* New York, NY: New Press.

Higgins, G. (1994). *Resilient adults: Overcoming a cruel past.* San Francisco, CA: Jossey-Bass.

Hillard, A. (1991). Do we have the will to educate all children? *Educational Leadership 49*(1), 31-36.

Kohn, A. (1993, September). Choices for children: Why and how to let students decide. *Phi Delta Kappan.*

Lifton, R, (1994).*The protean self: Human resilience in an age of fragmentation.* New York, NY: Basic Books.

McLaughlin, M., & Talbert, J. (1993). *Contexts that matter for teaching and learning.* Stanford, CA: Stanford University Press.

Meier, D. (1995). *The power of their ideas.* Boston, MA: Beacon Press.

Mills, R. (1991). A new understanding of self: The role of affect, state of mind, self-understanding, and intrinsic motivation. *Journal of Experimental Education 60*(1), 67-81.

Noddings, N. (1988, December 7). Schools face crisis in caring. *Education Week*, p.32.

Polakow, V. (1995). Naming and blaming: Beyond a pedagogy of the poor. In B. Swadener, & S. Lubeck (Eds.), *Children and families at promise: Deconstructing the discourse of risk.* Albany, NY: State University of New York Press.

Rutter, M. (1984, March). Resilient children. *Psychology Today*, 57-65.

Rutter, M., Maughan, B., Mortimore, P., Ouston, J., & Smith, A. (1979). *Fifteen thousand hours.* Cambridge, MA: Harvard University Press.

Seligman, M. (1995). *The optimistic child.* Boston, MA: Houghton Mifflin.

Swadener, B., & Lubeck, S. (Eds.) (1995). *Children and families at promise: Deconstructing the discourse of risk.* Albany, NY: State University of New York Press.

Wehmiller, P. (1992). When the walls come tumbling down. *Harvard Educational Review 62*(3), 373-383.

Werner, E., & Smith, R. (1989). *Vulnerable but invincible: A longitudinal study of resilient children and youth.* New York, NY: Adams, Bannister, and Cox.

Werner, E., & Smith, R. (1992). *Overcoming the odds: High-risk children from birth to adulthood.* New York, NY: Cornell University Press.

Werner, E. (1996, Winter). How children become resilient: Observations and cautions. *Resiliency In Action*, 18-28.

Bonnie Benard, M.S.W., has authored numerous articles and papers on resiliency. She can be reached at Resiliency Associates, 1238 Josephine, Berkeley, CA 94703, (p/f 510-528-4344), or by e-mail: bbenard@flashnet.com.

How to Support Turnaround Teachers

The characteristics and beliefs of turnaround teachers can be amplified when they are supported by colleagues and administration staff in a school building or organization. The following suggestions can help create classrooms, schools, and programs that are more likely to help students turn their lives around from risk to resilience. [Editors' note: These recomendations can easily be applied to other youth-serving programs.)

Reflect on and discuss as a staff your beliefs about innate resilience. What does it mean in our classrooms and schools if *all* kids are resilient? Answering this question as an individual and then coming to a consensus on the answer as a staff is the first step in creating a classroom or school that taps into its students' resilience.

Form a resiliency study group. Read the research on resiliency, including the studies of successful city schools. Share stories—both personal and literary—of individuals who successfully overcame the odds. "It is important to read about struggles that leads to empowerment and to successful advocacy, for resilient voices are critical to hear within the at-risk wasteland" (Polakow, 1995, p. 269). When working against the dominant risk paradigm, we need the support and "shelter of each other."

Focus on Climate. Schools and classrooms that have been turnaround experiences for stressed young people are continually described as being like "a family," "a home," "a community"—even "a sanctuary." "School was my church, my religion. It was constant, the only thing that I could count on every day.... I would not be here if it was not for school" (Children's Express, 1993). Creating these safe havens requires a collective focus on building inclusive communities through relationships and responsibilities that invite back our disconnected and disenfranchised youth—and their families.

Foster school-community collaboration to coordinate needed services for children and families. Meeting the needs of the whole child necessitates school, family, and community collaboration. Develop a list of community agencies, including after-school neighborhood-based organizations. Match the needs of your students and families with the services of these organizations.

Provide for teachers what students need. Nurturing and sustaining a belief in resilience is not only the critical task of teachers; it should be the main focus of administrators. Resilience applies to all of us. What has sustained youth in the face of adversity is equally what enables teachers and administrators to overcome the incredible stresses they face in schools today. Teachers need the same good stuff as their students: caring relationships with colleagues; positive beliefs, expectations, and trust on the part of the administration; and ongoing opportunities to reflect, engage in dialogue, and make decisions together. A wise administrator once remarked, "If you don't feed the teachers, they'll eat the students." Research has shown that providing teachers with the time and opportunity to work collegially together, and through this to build a sense of professional community, is critical in both sustaining school efforts and raising students' academic scores (McLaughlin & Talbert, 1993).

Self-assess. Make an assessment tool from the best practices describing turnaround teachers and schools. Assess your classroom and school and ask your students to do the same. Identify both areas of strength and areas of challenge.

Lessons from My Life: No More "Children At Risk"... All Children are "At Promise"

by Mervlyn Kitashima

What follows is an edited version of a speech Mervlyn Kitashima gave on July 1, 1997 at the University of Maryland. Her presentation was part of the Kaiser Permanente's annual "Building Hope: Exploring Resiliency in Youth and Communities" conference, and her audience was about 650 adult and youth conference attendees. She eloquently detailed her own life journey, as one of the 700 babies born on the island of Kauai studied by Emmy Werner and Ruth Smith for more than 40 years, from poverty and abuse and family alcoholism to stability and mental and emotional health. The lessons she shared are lessons for all who want to know "what really makes a difference" in the lives of children and youth.

Some years ago, I was sitting in a workshop and [the speaker] said there was this study done on the island of Kauai of all the babies born in 1955. I thought, "My golly, I was born on Kauai in 1955, so I guess that's me." It sparked my curiosity, so I said, "Mom, what is this all about?" She told me that when she was pregnant with me they were asked to participate in a study, and this study followed all of the children born on that island in 1955. I'm not sure why they came to Kauai except maybe it's small enough that it was doable. There were only 700 children born in the whole year. Social, cultural, economic situations, I guess, fit what they needed.

Then I remember when I was 18 years old, I got a survey in the mail. (Some of the study was done by written surveys.) The survey said, "If you fill this out for us, we'll give you $25." I said, "I can use $25." So I filled out the survey and sent it in. I had no idea what it was for. When I was 32 years old, I got a phone call from a Dr. Ruth Smith, and she said she wanted to come and interview. In Hawaii, we call it "talk story." She wanted to come and talk story. She said, "If you let me come, I'll give you $30." I said, "I can use $30." So she came, and we had a wonderful discussion. She's a lovely, lovely lady who still lives on Kauai.

[A few years ago] I was asked to sit on a panel at a conference we do in Hawaii every year. The topic was, "What made a difference for you?" Nobody had ever asked me that before. Nobody had ever said, "Merv, what made a difference for you? Why are you here and why do you do what you do?" It caused me to think about that. It made me go back. The second question I had to ask myself is, "Why did something have to make a difference for me?" As I started to look at this, I realized that there were things that went on in my growing up that, my golly, something really had to have made a difference for me. Because looking at this whole list of at risk factors, I should be totally whacked. I should be totally messed up. I realized that somewhere along the line something made a difference.

I want to share three things before I go on. Number one, my story is not unique. Number two, I share this with you with the permission of my family. When I found myself going all over the state and then into different parts of the country, I thought I'd better let my mother know what I [was] doing because I'm going to share with you stuff that most families choose not to share. I said, "Mom, this is what I've been asked to do. Is it okay?" And she said to me, "If it will help make a difference for somebody else, you have my blessing." So I do this with the permission and blessing of my family. Number three, I would like for us to change our whole concept of this idea of "at risk." I think when we label, what we do is we put people—families, children, youth—in what Hawaiians calls a *puka*. A *puka* is a hole or slot. As we label each other, ourselves, or the people we serve as "at risk," we put them in a place that perhaps will be very difficult to get out of. I want us to change that whole concept to no longer [speaking of] children, or youth, or families as "at risk," to [talking about] children, and youth, and families "at promise." I believe with every ounce of my body and soul that every child, adult, every human being has promise, is given the help to find their potential. Every single one of us has a place to go, a promise to be fulfilled.

> *"As we label each other, ourselves, or the people we serve as "at risk," we put them in a place that perhaps will be very difficult to get out of. I want us to change that whole concept to no longer [speaking of] children, or youth, or families as 'at risk,' to [talking about] children, and youth, and families 'at promise.' I believe with every ounce of my body and soul that every child, adult, every human being has promise, is given the help to find their potential. Every single one of us has a place to go, a promise to be fulfilled."*

Why Did Something Have to Make a Difference for Me?

Now, [my] story: When I started to think [about] why did something have to make a difference for Merv, I came up with a list. The first one on top of the list was—for where I was at that time in my life growing up on the island of Kauai— I was culturally wrong. My mother is Hawaiian, born and raised on the island, and my father is from New Jersey. Where I grew up was what we call Hawaiian Home; it's similar to the idea of your Native American Reservation. This land is designated for Hawaiians; you must be Hawaiian to live there and you even have an opportunity to have a home. But I wasn't Hawaiian; half of me was, and the other half was something that was not normal in that time. This was back in [the] early 60s. Though Hawaii is the melting pot of the world today, and there's a mixture of all kinds of cultures and people and ethnicity, they didn't mix back then. The Hawaiians stayed in one place; the Japanese stayed in one place; the Chinese stayed in one place; the Filipinos stayed in one place. So when we came along, people didn't know how to treat us. We were different. We looked different. We weren't Caucasian, or White, or *haole*, the Hawaiian word for foreigner, and we weren't Hawaiian. We were different, so we were culturally wrong. And we were treated differently.

> *"Not only was I this strange looking girl with the* haole *father, but now [I'm] the strange looking girl with the* haole *father whose mother is nuts. That's what I was in elementary school. And it became a difficult thing to deal with."*

Number two, we lived in a blended family. My mother had three children from a first marriage. My father had six children from a first marriage. Then they proceeded to have four more. And I was the oldest of the four. It created some difficulties, just the idea of the blending of families. The six of my father's children were here in the states and in all of my life, and I'm 42 years old, I have met only one of those six brothers and sisters. It is, again, a *puka*—a void—for me that I have family here that I don't even know. But I understand that it was a very bitter and ugly divorce so, there was no connection. [This] brings me to a real important point about children and families "at promise," especially children. They don't know what goes on in the adult lives of the people who care for them. All we know is this is our life and this is what we've got to deal with. So the blended family created its difficulties.

Number three, we were poor. I'm not sure why because my father was military. That's why he was on Kauai. He was in the military, and he had a paycheck, and he did go to work. But we didn't have anything. There were times when there was no food on the table. We never, ever, ever had new clothes, never. I cannot remember a time going to elementary school with a brand new dress. We never had shoes. It's a good thing in Hawaii you don't need them; it doesn't get cold enough. Bare feet are fine, and that's how we existed. If

> *"I cannot remember a time going to elementary school with a brand new dress. We never had shoes. It's a good thing in Hawaii you don't need them!"*

we were lucky, we had "flip flops." We call them rubber slippers. If we were lucky, we had a new pair of rubber slippers that may have cost 20 cents from the Ben Franklin store. [We] never had the things that we were supposed to have.

I don't know how it is here, but at home in the beginning of the year they have this long list of supplies that students need to bring to school. If you don't have food on your table, and you don't have clothes to wear, do you think you have money to buy all those supplies? No. So, you walk into the classroom and from day one, not only are you at a deficit because you look different and you sound different, but because you don't have everything you need, somebody is on your case for what you don't have. And again, it wasn't my fault. I had no clue why. It was just that this is the way it was.

Number four in my list of "at promise" characteristics: My father was an alcoholic. When he wasn't working, he was drunk. And when he was drunk, mom was angry. Lucky for us, mom didn't drink. The difficulties that came from an alcoholic father in our home created some stuff that I would hope most young people don't have to experience, but I know they do. My mother would rage when dad was drunk. I remember walking into the kitchen one day where she had grabbed his bottles, and busted [them], and was going after him. There was blood all over the kitchen, and there was blood all over her. As children, you don't stick around to watch your parents hurt each other. You take off. For us, because we lived on an island and in the country, we took off into the cane fields. We took off down to the beach. We took off into the mountains—wherever we could go, because you don't stick around. I remember watching my mother chase my father down with the car. He was drunk. She was angry, and she chased him with the car through the pasture fence, knocked him over. I don't know how the man lived to die a natural death, but he did.

> *"We were expected as children to work, and we were expected to work hard."*

I remember a time when I was in the second grade when my mother was institutionalized because she had a nervous breakdown. What was very difficult for me was the elementary school was [on] a little one-lane road, and the hospital was right across the street. So I would sit in my classroom and I would look out the window and know that my mother is over there. I didn't understand why she had to be there with all those funny people and why she couldn't go home. What else was very difficult was as wonderful as children are, they can be cruel in the things they say. Now, not only was I this strange looking girl with the *haole* father, but now [I'm] the strange looking girl with the *haole* father whose mother is nuts. That's what I was in elementary school. And it became a difficult thing to deal with.

So when I say I should be kind of whacky and messed up, maybe you can understand a little bit. I'm not. I'm pretty okay. You know, some people might argue that point, but I'm pretty okay. And so these things are not what is most important in my message to you today. It's the next part—the "what made a difference." How come I'm not messed up? How come I'm not whacked?

Out of the seven children who grew up in this Kauai home, six of us are really fine. There's only one, a sister two years older than I, who just has not been able to change it around. She has a major drug problem, homeless somewhere on the island. I have no clue where she is. [She's] been through [one] abusive relationship after another. Six out of seven, not bad. We love her

> *"Out of the seven children who grew up in this Kauai home, six of us are really fine."*

with all our heart and continue to hope for her and continue to be there whenever we can to help her pull it up.

How come the six of us are really basically okay? I can only share my understanding of what made a difference for me. I'm going to share four things. When I was asked, "What made a difference for you?," these were the four things I came up with. What's been very exciting is that it has fit into the research really nicely. I didn't learn about the research until a few years ago, and I hadn't paid attention to it until a few years ago. As I did learn more about it, it was exciting to me that it just fit.

The first thing that I think made a difference for me was we were expected as children to work, and we were expected to work hard. If we didn't, we would get lickings. We would get beat. That was all there was to it. If we didn't do our jobs, when mom and dad came home, we would get the belt or whatever was handy. We had a one acre piece of land, which is a lot for Hawaii. We had to take care of it. As children, we took care of the yard, the house, the clothes, each other, the cars. We did everything. My father cooked when there was something to cook, and my mother simply coped. I asked her one day, "Mom, what do you do?" Because we did everything. We did laundry by hand for nine people. If there's no food, there's no washing machine. If there's no food, there's no lawn mower to clean the yard. So we did it with sickles and hoes and what we call cane knives.

I remember once we were late. We had played too long with our friends, and mom and dad were on their way home and we hadn't done our jobs. So we decided to set fire to the yard to burn down the bush we were supposed to take care of. We thought that was the fastest way to do it and we didn't want to get the belt. So we burnt nearly the whole community down. I mean, the fire took care of what it was supposed to take of and then it went further and further, and all the neighbors came out with their water hoses, and we managed to get it under control. When mom and dad came home, it was already dark so they couldn't see the burnt backyard, so we didn't get the belt until the next day.

> "When things got rough, [I learned] to dig in my heels and say, 'How am I going to make this happen?' versus, 'This is too hard, I quit.' I think we're raising a generation of young people who say too quickly, 'This is too hard, I quit.' We need to give them opportunity to work."

Children do whatever it takes not to get the punishment. That's what I did. Like I told you, laundry by hand, scrubbing the floor, hands and knees. And if you missed one little spot, you'd get the belt and you did it again. If you missed one piece of food on the dish, you'd get the belt and [our father] dumped it back in the sink again. You did it over until it was done right. This made a difference for me. It doesn't sound like a wonderful opportunity, but what it did was [teach] me how to dig in my heels and work. When things got rough, [I learned] to dig in my heels and say, "How am I going to make this happen?" versus, "This is too hard, I quit." I think we're raising a generation of young people who say too quickly, "This is too hard, I quit." We need to give them opportunity to work.

I have seven kids. Not one of them comes to me and says, "Mom, I'd be happy to do the dishes for you today." But they have to because that's part of their responsibility. Work is a building block to better things. I didn't see it then. As a parent, I see it now. My children hate it, but they do it because they have no choice. I don't give them the belt. I have other ways to make sure it happens. The ability to work causes us to learn how to deal with the things that come, and that's what it did for me. It gave me the ability to dig in my heels and say, "How is this going to happen?"

One of the protective factors is chores and responsibilities. In the study that was done on the island of Kauai by Emmy Werner and Ruth Smith, one of the things they found [was] that the children who had responsibilities, the children who had chores at home, did better. So as adults, we need to provide opportunities for our children to be responsible, for them to lead,

> *"Probably the most important to me was caring and supportive people throughout all of my life. I was fortunate to have people. A lot of times it wasn't my parents because they were too busy needing to take care of their own stuff."*

for them to take charge. And as young people, we need to take charge, to grab a hold of that responsibility to lead.

Most Important: Caring and Supportive People

Number two, probably the most important to me was caring and supportive people throughout all of my life. I was fortunate to have people. A lot of times it wasn't my parents because they were too busy needing to take care of their own stuff. For me, the first and foremost as a child was my grandma. A lot of us have wonderful grandmas and grandpas and aunties and uncles. Mine was my Grandma Kahaunaele, which is my mother's mother. Grandma Kahaunaele lived just down the road from us, which made it nice.

Hawaii is red dirt. It's red dirt and it stains. It's terrible. When things got really bad at home, we would end up at Grandma and Grandpa Kahaunaele's home. My Grandma Kahaunaele was a wonderful, wonderful, quiet, Hawaiian woman. She had red hair and white skin. I'm not sure how that happened; it's one of those things they don't tell you about in your family history. She didn't say much. I don't remember her voice, but she had this incredible heart. I remember a couple of things you need to know. Number one is we were "those children." You know what "those children" are?—the ones where you as parents say to your own, "I don't want you playing with 'those children.' I don't want you going to 'those people's' house." We were the "those children" that nobody wanted around. I don't know if it's because we were different, or because we were always dirty, or because our clothes were always dirty. I don't know why, but we were. That's how I felt. My Grandma Kahaunaele never treated me like one of "those children." What you need to understand, however, is she was immaculately clean. Her house was spotless and shiny. She washed and ironed pillow cases, underwear, T-shirts. That's how she was. It was immaculate.

You can imagine what she thought when she saw us coming out of the cane field because we'd cut through the park, cut through the cane field. And if there was water in the irrigation ditches, we'd jump in there and catch toads and tadpoles and

> *"We were 'those children.' You know what 'those children' are?—the ones where you as parents say to your own, 'I don't want you playing with 'those children.' I don't want you going to 'those people's' house.' We were the 'those children' that nobody wanted around."*

whatever else there was. And then we ended up at her house. She must have said, "Oh my golly. Here they come." You know, I would have. I'm a grandma. I can understand this now. If she thought it, she never said

it, never said it to me. Not once do I remember her saying to me, "You are so filthy. Go home. I don't want you here." However, what she would do is she would dump us in the outside tub and wash off the red dirt and [then] let us in the house.

My Grandma Kahaunaele is the only person I remember who would comb my hair. I remember going to school one day and the teacher said to me, "Doesn't anybody ever comb your hair? Doesn't anybody ever wash your face?" I guess I was dirty. Grandma Kahaunaele was the only who would comb my hair. You know, Hawaiian girls always have long hair, and I had long hair, but it was always tangled, and it was always dirty. I remember sitting in the playground, first grade, and wondering why my head was so itchy. It's because it was so dirty. Back then I'd scratch and scratch. Grandma Kahaunaele was the one who would wash my hair, and she was the only one who would take the tangles out. She would sit me down at her knee and she'd have this giant, yellow comb. She'd patiently take every tangle out of my hair. And for any of you who've had long, tang-

> *"My Grandma Kahaunaele never treated me like one of 'those children.'… Not once do I remember her saying to me, 'You are so filthy. Go home. I don't want you here.'… [She] was the one who would wash my hair, and she was the only one who would take the tangles out."*

led hair, with a comb going through it, not fun, you know? Your head is yanking as it gets caught, and I'd be crying. She would say, "Almost *pau*, almost *pau*." *Pau* means finished. "Almost done." She would eventually get finished, and I remember feeling clean, and I remember feeling pretty, and I remember feeling like maybe somebody cares for me, even for just a little while.

My Grandma Kahaunaele had a wooden leg. When she was a child, a car ran over her toes. The infection grew and grew and grew until they cut her leg off just below her knee. In order to put her wooden leg on, she put [on] about six pairs of socks and then she'd buckle her leg right here. I can still [see] her doing it at the edge of her bed. At night when she would go to bed, she would take off the leg and take off the socks and stand it at the post of her bed. We spent many, many nights at Grandma and Grandpa Kahaunaele's home. When mom was in the institution, that's where we stayed because my father couldn't handle all of us.

I remember waking up at night, nightmares, and crying, and afraid, looking for someone to care for me. My vision that I will never forget is this woman crawling on her hands and knees down the hall to come and make sure that I was okay… because she had no leg. She took her leg off. Then when I was alright and settled and feeling better, she would crawl back to her room. An example, a memory, of caring and support unsurpassed by anything else for me.

Each of us needs to build into our own life and the lives of the people you service, this kind of caring and support, someone who will love you—or you be the one who will love somebody else—without condition, regardless [of] what they look like, how dirty they are, what kind of clothes they wear, the color of their skin, hair, or eyes. To love uncondition-

> *"My vision that I will never forget is this woman crawling on her hands and knees down the hall to come and make sure that I was okay… because she had no leg. She took her leg off. Then when I was alright and settled and feeling better, she would crawl back to her room. An example, a memory, of caring and support unsurpassed by anything else for me."*

ally—every single one of us needs this. It is one of the proven factors in the resiliency research: caring and supportive people and places.

I had a fifth grade math teacher, and I remember she said to me one day, "You are a good-for-nothing Hawaiian and will never amount to anything." Now, as 10 or 11-year-old you simply say, "Okay." You take that information and you store it. You store it in the back of your brain. Back then, if you answered back to your teacher, you'd get whacked from the principal. Then you'd go home and get whacked again from your parents. So you just take that information and you store it. At the same time in my life, I had a principal [who] said to me, "You are Hawaiian, and you can be anything you choose to be." Each one of these people said this to me once. I remember the tone. I remember the feeling of both. I remember the words. I remember everything about both situations.

I think I listened to Ron Martin, my principal. As I thought about this over these last few years, it had nothing to do with being Hawaiian. I'm sure he said to the Japanese student, "You are Japanese, and you can be anything you choose to be." "You are Filipino, and you can be anything you choose to be." It had to do with, this youngster needs me today. This youngster needs me to say something today to help her over the hump. And that's what he did. I will always be grateful for that.

For those of us who work with young people on a daily basis, beware of what we say, because it's remembered. If I were to ask you to remember some of the stuff that was said to you, can you remember the good and the bad? We remember the bad first, yeah? And then maybe a few of the good comes in. Know that what we communicate to

> *"I had to decide, am I a good-for-nothing Hawaiian? Or can I really be anything I choose to be?"*

our youngsters is valuable, and it will either build or destroy. As young people, we've got to decide which one we're going to believe. The Mrs. Math Teacher, good-for-nothing Hawaiian? I had to decide, am I a good-for-nothing Hawaiian? Or can I really be anything I choose to be?

How Education Made a Difference

Third thing—first was hard work, [second was] caring and supportive people—that made a difference for me was education. When I was 12 years old, I left Kauai and went to the main island of Oahu because there is a school there for Hawaiian kids. You must be Hawaiian to go to that school—all of the money comes from King Kamahamaha. His granddaughter, who had no children of her own, left all of her estate, lands, and moneys to the education of Hawaiian children. So we have the Kamahamaha schools, and I had the privilege of attending at age 12, seventh grade. Personally I would not send my child away at age 12. There's too much that goes on in the life of a 12-year-old. But for us it was one of the best things my parents did. When I asked my mom why she sent us, she said it was cheaper for them. That's the truth. They were struggling. Dad still had his alcohol problem. He was still gambling, all kinds of stuff. So to give us the opportunity to go away and be cared for and get an education was good for them.

> *"We need to be willing to take a risk for kids. It's not always easy. As adult service providers for them, we need to be willing to see differently, to change what is normal sometimes to help our youngsters over the hump."*

But more than that, what it did for me is it brought in the vision. It allowed me opportunity to participate in stuff I would not have done on the island of Kauai. It helped me to see that, my golly, I can do some things. It gave me choices and opportunities to see what I was good at. I got involved in student government. I got involved in music. I got involved in intramurals or athletics, as much as there was for females at that time. However, the "at promise" idea followed.

At age 16, as a junior in high school, I became pregnant. The policy at Kamahamaha schools was when you're pregnant, you're gone. I was taken to the office of the Dean of Students; her name was Wynona Reuben. Mrs. Reuben was a big lady and she had a man's voice. And if you were in her office, you were in trouble. I was in her office because I was in trouble, and she basically said, "Well, I'm sorry. You've got to leave." She put me on an airplane back to Kauai to tell my parents. I went home and I talked to mother, who was not happy.

We had to make some decisions. The decision at that time was that I would get married. So at age 16, I got married. At age 17, I had my first child. We came back to Oahu because that's where my husband-to-be lived, and he [had] just graduated from high school. We went [back] to Kamahamaha schools and they said, "Sorry, you're out of here."

So my mother took me to a school in downtown Honolulu. It was a special education school. There's mainstreaming now, but back then there wasn't. It was for special needs children from all ages. We walked into this school and it was green and wooden and [had] broken windows that had boards on them. It was, in my perception, not a good place. [It] had children in wheelchairs and babies up to what looked like adults who were [disabled] mentally, physically, emotionally, severely to mildly, all kinds. It was terrifying. I looked at

> *"When I went away, I realized that it wasn't the way it had to be. There were people who had fathers who didn't drink. I realized that I could make choices."*

that, and in tears I turned to my mom and said, "Mom if this is what a high school diploma means, I don't need it. I cannot do this. I cannot be here." And so we left.

We went back up [to] Wynona Reuben's office. I don't know how or what happened, but I was allowed to go back to school, pregnant and married. Never happened at this institution before. A few years ago, I wanted to find out what [had] happened, so I called my counselor who was still counseling at that school. I said, "Tom, how come they let me come back?" He said Wynona Reuben called the counseling department—they had been looking at this idea of teenage pregnancy of students—and she said to them: "You know the parent/student program that we've been talking about? I want you to push it, and I want this student to be the first one in it. She is not a bad student. She made a mistake."

Sometimes we look at the youngsters who make mistakes as bad, and we're not. We're not bad. We just need help in getting back to what is right. She was the help. Now, in this institution called Kamahamaha schools, it is not easy to make change. I had teachers who refused to have me in their class because I was pregnant and because I was married. One of "those children" again. "These kinds of students do not belong at Kamahamaha." I was not allowed into some of the classes. There were others who were ready for the change. What made the difference here was this Wynona Reuben who was willing to take a risk for kids, to go out on a major limb to change something that was not popular, on behalf of kids. It wasn't on behalf of me; it was on behalf of everyone before me and after me who would be in the same place.

We need to be willing to take a risk for kids. It's not always easy. As adult service providers for them, we need to be willing to see differently, to change what is normal sometimes to help our youngsters over the hump. That's what she did for me. Intermixed into the broadening of the vision was the caring and support from someone who I didn't even think cared a rip about us, but she did.

> *"Somewhere, someplace down the line, somebody had taught me, 'There is somebody greater than us who loves you.' And that was my hope and my belief."*

The other thing that going away to Kamahamaha did for me was it broadened the vision a whole lot. It helped me make some choices that I never knew I could. [On Kauai] all around me in my community was alcoholism and abuse. Uncle Sonny across the way, every day, all day long, he sat on his porch with his bottle of primo beer. Uncle Henry next door was a policeman but when he got angry, he would beat his children. I remember one day his littlest son came out with an iron burn on his back because his dad was

"So, at age 16, I got married....At age 17, I had my first child.... I should mention that my teenage husband, 18-years-old at the time [we married], is still my husband of 26 years."

angry at him. All around me, that's what I saw. In my own home, that's what I saw, and I thought that's the way life has to be. When I went away, I realized that it wasn't the way it had to be. There were people who had fathers who didn't drink. I realized that I could make choices.

It was there, when I was a student at Kamahamaha, that I promised myself I would never date or marry anybody who drank. I saw what alcohol did to my mother; it destroyed her. The alcohol [also] destroyed [my father]. I remember seeing my father passed out in his urine and vomit. And I refused to have that in my life, I made that choice. That is not something I wanted for me or for my children. And I've been able to keep true to that promise to myself.

I should mention that my teenage husband, 18-years-old at the time [we married], is still my husband of 26 years. He's a pretty neat guy. He's a school teacher. He's been teaching for 21 of those 26 years, and it was because of people who cared about us who helped us get through those beginning times. So allowing for choices, participation, and involvement that broadens vision—that was number three.

My Belief in "Something Greater"

The fourth thing that made a difference for me—when there was no Grandma Kahaunaele, when there was no Ron Marsh, when there was no Wynona Reuben, [or] the many, many others—was that somewhere, someplace down the line, somebody had taught me, "There is somebody greater than us who loves you." And that was my hope and my belief. Whatever that translates for you—a belief in a God, a belief in a religion, a goal, a dream, something that we can all hang on to. As adults, we need to give our young people hope and something to hang on to. As young people, we need to find our own.

Treasures exist in each one of our children—be they our own or somebody else's—and we need to be patient until they realize their promise. We need to be caring and supportive, and we need to provide opportunities for work and involvement and participation until they realize their promise. That's my message to you: Never give up on kids. Kids, never give up on yourselves... never.

Mervlyn Kitashima is district coordinator for the Parent-Community Networking Centers in Hawaii's Department of Education, and she has developed curriculum and training for Hawaii school administrators, educators, and parents. She can be contacted at her workplace by phone (808-453-6460) or by fax (808-456-4385).

It Takes a Child to Raise a Whole Village

by John P. Kretzmann, Ph.D., and Paul H. Schmitz

The following chapter originally appeared in the 1994-95 issue of Wingspread, *a newsletter of The Johnson Foundation. It has been edited to fit the format of this book and is reprinted with permission from the authors.*

All photographs are reprinted from Reform, Resiliency, and Renewal • Kids in Action, *published by KIDS Consortium in cooperation with the Edmund S. Muskie School of Public Service at the University of Southern Maine and the Center for Educational Media.*

Children and villages. Villages and children. In recent years, lots of people have been rethinking their relationships to each other. The cliched rendition, usually attributed to African origins and now almost a mantra, has obviously struck a responsive chord. It *does* take a whole village—not just parents, schools, or child-care and child-development professionals—to raise kids. The invitation for a broader commitment to young people is clearly welcome and long overdue.

> **"Contrary to media stories that state again and again how apathetic youth are, young people have been organizing themselves as contributors to our communities."**

But the cliche is incomplete at best. It still leaves us with a set of assumptions about young people that we believe are historically unprecedented and powerfully destructive. In the cliche, people (adults) in villages act to "raise" young people. Young folks are the objects of the action, never the subjects. They are passive and useless. They are defined as deficient—of knowledge, of skills, of any useful capacities—and relegated with their cohorts to the filling stations we call schools. The assumption is that, magically, at age 18 or 21, young people will emerge from their years of being filled, and re-enter the community as full and useful contributors.

This formula is a disaster. Not only has it produced a generation of young people who think of themselves as useless, but it also has isolated that generation from productive interaction with older generations. It has relegated more than a third of American citizens to inaction or worse and has deprived youth of the experience necessary for fulfilling their roles as citizens and contributors to the community.

Villages suffer when there is a failure to empower all members of society, but especially when there is no empowerment of those who represent the nation's future. Clearly, individuals and communities need to re-examine how they view young people and their role in our society.

Rather than passive vessels to be filled during the first 18 years of life, children can be key members of communities. Whether "A" students or dropouts, all-star athletes or suburban skateboarders, young people can help raise villages when they are seen as individuals with skills and capacities, with ideas and enthusiasm. For villages to be whole, young people must be valued.

Young people who contribute to raising villages come in a range of ages—from young kids of six to young adults of 26. These are not young people who fit media stereotypes—they are anything but apathetic, uncaring, dumb, violent, and lost. They are, in fact, gifted, skilled, and resourceful. And they are ready to contribute their gifts in all communities.

Recently, a coalition of Wisconsin foundations, including the Johnson Foundation, convened focus groups of young people and adults who "serve" young people. Not surprisingly, the survey found that perceptions diverged. On one hand, the adults worried about all of the needs and problems that young people had and how adults could remedy them. The young folks, on the other hand, focused on their desire to contribute, to do more. They expressed strong yearning for purpose, for meaning, for ways to be useful to the wider community, especially in nonpatronizing, intergenerational efforts. These values far outstripped their yearning for material things—the stereotype most often associated with youth desires.

There is a disconnect here between what adults perceive young people need and what young people really want. Adults have fallen into the habit of expecting too little of young people when, all the while, they want to shake off pessimism and contribute their gifts and talents. Communities abound with opportunities for young people to contribute, but their participation is too often marginalized and tokenized.

Young people have the gifts and talents to raise their villages. They lack only the confidence of their villages in them to do it.

What to do: Fortunately for everyone, young people them-selves are taking the initiative to

> *"Villages suffer when there is a failure to empower all members of society, but especially when there is no empowerment of those who represent the nation's future."*

"Ten Commandments" for Involving Young People in Community Building

by John P. Kretzmann

1. Always start with the gifts, talents, knowledge, and skills of young people—never with their needs and problems.

2. Always lift up the unique individual, never the category to which the young person belongs. It is "Frank, who sings so well" or "Maria, the great soccer player," never the "at-risk youth" or the "pregnant teen."

3. Share the conviction that (a) every community is filled with useful opportunities for young people to contribute to the community, and (b) there is no community institution or association that can't find a useful role for young people.

4. Try to distinguish between real community building work, and games or fakes—because young people know the difference.

5. Fight—in every way you can—age segregation. Work to overcome the isolation of young people.

6. Start to get away from the principle of aggregation of people by their emptiness. Don't put everyone who can't read together in the same room. It makes no sense.

7. Move as quickly as possible beyond youth "advisory boards" or councils, especially those boards with only one young person on them.

8. Cultivate many opportunities for young people to teach and to lead.

9. Reward and celebrate every creative effort, every contribution made by young people. Young people can help take the lead here.

10. In every way possible, amplify this message to young people: *We need you!* Our community cannot be strong and complete without you.

redefine their relationships with the rest of the village. In community after community, young people are reasserting their identity as subjects and actors, as people with a broad range of capacities and resources to contribute to the well-being of their villages.

In fact, contrary to media stories that state again and again how apathetic youth are, young people have been organizing themselves as contributors to communities. They have started groups such as Public Allies, Youth on Board, the Youth Volunteer Corps, Campus Opportunity Outreach League, Funds for the Community's Future, GreenCorps, City Year, Teach for America, *Who Cares* magazine, and many others—all national organizations run by young adults.

Public Allies, an organization founded at a Wingspread conference four years ago, places young leaders from diverse backgrounds, "Allies," in community service apprenticeships in six cities throughout the United States. The Allies work full-time, four days a week, taking on specific challenges with significant responsibilities at nonprofit organizations, schools, and government agencies. On

"Rather than passive vessels to be filled during the first 18 years of life, children can be key members of communities."

the fifth day of each week, the Allies come together for leadership and professional training and to design and implement team-service projects to improve the community: Public Allies empowers young people to empower others—to raise villages.

Here are sketches of four young people who have helped to raise their villages.

• Angel was released from a five-year prison sentence at the age of 21. He began reading while in prison and began college soon after his release. He also began volunteering at a local youth center that was surrounded by gang activity. He began building relationships with children in the neighborhood, showing them the choices they had and the consequences of their actions. Today, Angel is a part-time student who works with first-time juvenile offenders through a county government initiative, helping them to find their talents and to pursue them.

• Dan grew up in a well-to-do suburb and began attending a private college. During a summer break, he was struck by a news story about discrimination against kids with HIV. The next summer, he worked with a few friends to start a summer camp for HIV-infected and affected children. During the rest of the year, Dan served as a health educator at a Boys and Girls Club. Dan is currently working to start a new program to provide community service opportunities and leadership training for teenagers infected and affected by the HIV virus.

• Carmella was a recipient of multiple social services while growing up. One of them, the foster care system, placed her at a boarding school, which dropped her off at the Salvation Army at the age of 18. Homeless, and with no family, Carmella began volunteering at her homeless shelter, while finishing her high school diploma. Carmella's courage and tenacity led her to become a board member of a grass-roots advocacy organization; to be the first woman selected for the city's midnight basketball league; and to be adopted by the volunteer director of a homeless advocacy group. As an Ally, Carmella organized a youth council in the housing development where she played basketball. The council suggested to city leaders ways in which the housing development could be improved for residents. The young people also created a video about their lives in the development. Carmella is now finishing college and continuing to work full time with young people.

- Leif decided upon college graduation to contribute his skills to his community. He was asked to create an economic development arm of a neighborhood group in one of the city's poorest neighborhoods. Leif began optimistically and in 10 months initiated a job placement program that helped 60 residents in the work force, created a thriving business association, and organized two neighborhood service days. For three months, he and a team of Public Allies identified neighborhood residents' capacities, and then mobilized more than 250 volunteers— most of them neighborhood residents—for the service days. These local people, with their children, came out to rehab homes, clean vacant lots, change storms and screens for the elderly, plant community gardens, and perform other neighborhood improvement tasks during neighborhood service days. Leif now works for Public Allies, leading a team of Allies working on economic and neighborhood development.

"In fact, so many young people want to contribute that many facilitating organizations are hard pressed to meet the demand."

In each case, these young people contributed to the community by helping others—especially other young people—discover their capacities and contribute. But involving young people is not just a "good" thing for them, keeping them busy doing "good" things. These young people and those they touch are learning what it means to be members of a village, to be citizens. They are invigorating the life of

Young people not only *want* to be involved in the life of their community, they *already* are involved through many groups and organizations they have began on their own. Following is a brief list of groups founded or run by youth.

City Year
11 Stillings St.
Boston, MA 02210
617-927-2500
www.cityyear.org

Dudley St. Neighborhood Initiative
513 Dudley St.
Roxbury, MA 02119
617-442-9670
www.urbanvillage@dsni.org
Through its youth group, called Nubian Roots, DSNI involves young people in community planning and development.

Strive Incorporated/Teen Forum
1737 N. Palmer, Suite 200
Milwaukee, WI 53202
414-374-3511
www.strivemediainstitute.com
www.mygumbo.com
This organization involves high school students who produce, anchor, and report for a weekly TV news magazine on the local ABC affiliate, and provides young writers with opportunities to edit sections and write for local newspapers. They also provide summer-long financial training workshops for teens. They have also recently begun publishing *My Gumbo*, a magazine by teens for teens.

Youth as Resources
1000 Connecticut Ave., NW, 13th Fl.
Washington, D.C. 20036
202-261-4131
www.yar@ncpc.org
This program, which can be run by community organizations, foundations, or coalitions, encourages youth involvement by awarding small grants to youth-run community projects. Proposals for the grants are reviewed by an advisory board comprised of both youth and adults. YAR also publishes a free quarterly newsletter.

Youth Enterprises Network
c/o Bethel New Life
367 N. Karlov
Chicago, IL 60624
773-826-5540
www.bethelnewlife.org
Youth Enterprises Network involves highschool students on the west side of Chicago in starting businesses and creating jobs in a community with high unemployment.

Public Allies
1511 K St., N.W.
Washington, D.C. 20005
202-638-3300
www.publicallies.org

this nation and creating a foundation of leadership that is essential for the future of its democracy.

These are not isolated stories. We know of hundreds of young people like Angel, Dan, Carmella, and Leif. In fact, so many young people want to contribute that many facilitating organizations are hard pressed to meet the demand.

The demand can be met in communities by changing their relationships with children. It is now incumbent upon *every* local community to reopen itself to the gifts of its young people.

In fact, some communities have begun by constructing "opportunity inventories," extensive listings of all the ways in which young people already contribute, and the additional opportunities awaiting them. As part of these inventories, young people are invited to the table and asked about the opportunities they see to contribute their gifts and talents.

This is but one method of sending the message clearly and concretely to all of the young people in our villages: "Our village desperately *needs* you: without your contributions, we cannot be whole." ➤

According to recent surveys, young people, ages 13 to 17, are helping to "raise villages" in the following ways:

1. interviewing community leaders
2. drawing land-use and planning maps
3. devising a development strategy with new businesses
4. "shadowing," then advising executives
5. writing "walking tour" guide books
6. building a Halloween graveyard on a vacant lot
7. starting and operating a credit union
8. leading community cooking classes

9. building displays for businesses
10. conducting oral history interviews
11. writing and publishing an ethnic history of the school and neighborhood
12. painting murals in the community
13. rehabbing apartments; building affordable housing
14. repairing pipe organs
15. beginning union apprenticeships
16. organizing to save a public library

17. making and selling place mats for restaurants
18. publishing a neighborhood newspaper
19. mediating racial disputes
20. developing an adult literacy program
21. processing recyclables
22. producing and reporting for a weekly TV news program
23. creating dance troupes that perform at community events
24. emceeing community events
25. designing t-shirts for neighborhood groups and events

26. using technology skills to assist non-profits and houses of worship
27. observing youth-serving agencies and working with foundations to create incentives for more meaningful youth involvement, and then influencing gift decisions

"The young folks ... focused on their desire to contribute, to do more. They expressed strong yearning for purpose, for meaning, for ways to be useful to the wider community, especially in non-patronizing, intergenerational efforts."

John P. Kretzmann is director of the Neighborhood Innovations Network at the Center for Urban Affairs and Policy Research at Northwestern University. He is the coauthor of the book, Building Communities from the Inside Out. *Kretzmann has been a participant at Wingspread conferences and was a featured speaker at a 1995 Wingspread Briefing.*

Paul H. Schmitz is founder and director of the Milwaukee office of Public Allies. While an undergraduate at University of Wisconsin-Milwaukee, Schmitz attended a Wingspread conference as a Wingspread Fellow. Through his participation in the Fellows program, he was introduced to the national founder of Public Allies.

Federal, State, and Local Funding to "Develop Resiliency": Four Important Issues

by Nan Henderson, M.S.W.

I have been receiving reports from excited friends and colleagues about federal funding for various "resiliency-focused" initiatives. It seems that requests for proposals (RFPs) are increasingly using the term "resilience," and including various references to developing resilience as a goal, in conjunction with promoting effective education, violence prevention, and the prevention of other risk behaviors. That federal agencies are, to any degree, using resiliency language and citing resiliency research is good news. In addition, the newly stated requirements that federal funding be directed to approaches that have evaluated efficacy has long been needed.

These new developments are steps in the right direction, and should be celebrated! To be true to the body of resiliency research, however, federal (and state and local) funding agencies with the goal of fostering resiliency need to address some additional issues as next steps toward realizing that goal:

 Issue #1: Are additional programs and/or layers of bureaucracy really needed to meet the goal of increased youth resilience?

In reading through one of the new "developing resilience" RFPs, I was struck that it required yet another programmatic structure, potentially involving a newly convened group of "community stakeholders." I juxtaposed this approach to dispersing monies to develop resilience with the clearly scientifically documented resiliency-bolstering impact of the Big Brothers/Big Sisters program, which currently has a waiting list of thousands of youth, with the majority on that list being boys, and a large number of those, African American boys. (For details of the Big Brother/Big Sister

> *"To be true to the body of resiliency research, federal (and state and local) funding agencies with the goal of fostering resiliency need to address some additional issues as next steps toward realizing that goal."*

evaluation, see chapter one). Federal agencies thrive on starting programs, which are sometimes needed, but in the case of fostering resiliency, a better approach might be to simply channel money into organizations already in place that have documented success. In the case of the Big Brothers/Big Sisters program, and additional mentoring programs with documented efficacy noted by Emmy Werner in the Foreword of this book, no other prevention approach I am aware of has shown such high levels of success in reducing violence, drug use, alcohol use, as well as improving school attendance, grade point average, and family and other relationships. With the success evident, and the need great for more funding, it seems that monies that are available should first be applied to what is in place that does work. Werner also notes in her Foreword:

> Research on resilient children and youth has repeatedly shown that if a parent is incapacitated or unavailable, other significant people can play an enabling [resilience] role in a youngster's life, whether they are grandparents, older siblings, stable child care providers, competent and responsible peers, teachers, elder mentors, or youth workers. In many communities, it may make better sense to strengthen such informal ties to kith and kin than to introduce additional layers of bureaucracy into the delivery of services, and it might be less costly as well.

Conclusion: The first question to be answered in directing funds to achieve the goal of increased youth resiliency is, "Are there existing approaches in place in a school or community with documented efficacy that need funding?" A second question to guide funding: "Are there ways to use this money to strengthen informal ties to all the positive 'surrogates' or potential 'surrogates' in young people's lives?"

 Issue #2: Is it enough to insert "resilience" into what are essentially RFPs to reduce risk behaviors?

As Shirley Trout stated in her article, "A Strength Approach to Adolescent Development" in the January/February 1999 issue of *Resiliency In Action*, "Positive statements about adolescents are usually worded as improvements in problem behaviors, rather than identified from a criteria that delineates optimal functioning" (p.4). The Wolins (1994) agree, noting in their video *Survivor's Pride* that in the widely accepted "medical model" of health (from which risk factor research originates), "health is defined as the absence of illness, rather than the presence of something positive."

> *"Federal agencies thrive on starting programs, which are sometimes needed, but in the case of fostering resiliency, a better approach might be to simply channel money into organizations already in place that have documented success."*

The RFPs for promoting resilience I have seen to date seem to be an attempt to insert the term resilience into a risk-focused approach to adolescent wellness. One of these had a 19-item risk factor chart and pages of discussion of risks for youth violence, with a much less complete identification of protective factors (no chart included) and of the process of promoting protection as a route to resiliency, including the reduction of violent behavior.

Conclusion: "Developing resilience" involves more than just reducing risk behaviors. Approaches funded should target the reduction of not one, but the web of risk behaviors, since research (Resnick, et al. 1997) clearly shows they are all connected, as well as the increase of positive measures of adolescent wellness (such as pro-social relationships, improved school performance, contributions to community, and positive expectations for one's future).

(3) **Issue # 3: Since fostering resilience occurs primarily through person-to-person interactions that involve a specific attitude of unconditional caring and belief in another's capacity to overcome adversity (Werner & Smith, 1992; Higgins, 1994; Wolin quoted in Benard, 1999), how will the development of this attitude be addressed?**

The heart of fostering resiliency, as documented to date, is the quality of person-to-person relationships. Werner and Smith found in their on-going 45-year Kauai study that "the person was more important than the program," and that the programs that assisted the most were those that provided support similar to an extended family (Werner, 1993). It is interesting to note that the most successful resiliency development programs, are all person-to-person mentoring approaches. Funding for the goal of fostering resilience must address the current widely prevalent attitude that young people's risks are more powerful than their capacity for positive adaptation and change or else those involved in any "resiliency programming" may not provide this most crucial component of fostering resiliency. The current U.S. culture is one obsessed with deficits and weaknesses, and recent Gallup polls document that most adults think today's young people are too damaged and inadequate to successfully take the reigns of the future. Kids complain that adults view them as troublemakers when-

> *"Funding for the goal of fostering resilience must address the current widely prevalent attitude that young people's risks are more powerful than their capacity for positive adaptation and change or else those involved in any 'resiliency programming' may not provide this most crucial component of fostering resiliency."*

ever they are in stores, restaurants, or malls (*USA Today*, 1998). An inadvertent (but very debilitating to the process of resiliency) side effect of the past decade's emphasis on "youth at risk" is the common belief that most young people are packages of risks waiting to disintegrate.

The reality is just the opposite. "Most adolescents are doing well," was the conclusion of researchers who are conducting the Congressionally-mandated, National Longitudinal Study of Adolescent Health (Add Health), the largest scientific study of adolescents ever conducted in this country (Add Health, 1997). Furthermore, the body of resilience research documents that the majority of young people with many risks, and even those engaging in risk behaviors, do eventually rebound to wellness—by their own self-report and by the report of close family members, employers, and teachers.

Conclusion: Funding for approaches to foster resiliency must include strategies to address the prevalent negative attitudes about young people and their capacity to bounce back so that those implementing these approaches communicate the all-important resiliency-fostering attitude of optimism, caring despite past behaviors, and belief in the capacity for positive transformation.

 Issue #4: Is it important that funding for adolescent wellness include requirements for "walking the resiliency talk" of providing young people with opportunities for meaningful involvement, i.e. involving kids in every aspect of program planning and implementation?

Rodney Skager, a Professor Emeritus of UCLA's Graduate School of Education, has criticized the new Safe and Drug-Free Schools guidelines (for dispensing the program's more than $500 million) because they don't include a requirement of student involvement and participation (Alexander, 1999)."Developing resilience" RFPs I have seen from other federal agencies are also lacking this requirement. Since they often quote Bonnie Benard's (1991) synthesis of resiliency research as showing that "providing opportunities for meaningful participation" is one of three *crucial* protective conditions, it is ironic these RFPs don't even mention the desirability of youth involvement—much less include a requirement that this happen.

> *"The data may in fact one day show that including youth in the process of program conception and implementation was ultimately the most powerful aspect of prevention programming. The need for this requirement is especially apparent in funding programs designed to 'develop resilience' since this has been documented as one of three crucial resiliency development strategies."*

Conclusion: Young people are hungry to share their gifts; schools, communities, and, certainly, all programs for fostering resiliency are in critical need of youth input and participation. When this becomes the norm in all youth program funding, the data may in fact one day show that including youth in the process of program conception and implementation was ultimately the most powerful aspect of prevention programming.

The need for this requirement is especially apparent in funding programs designed to "develop resilience" since this has been documented as one of three crucial resiliency development strategies. ➤

References

Add Health. (1997). *Strong family, school relationships protect teens from violence, substance abuse, and more* (news release, September 10, 1997). Bethesda: MD: Add Health, Burness Communications.

Alexander, B. (1999). New guidelines to target lame programs get groans and growls. *Youth Today 8* (3), 22-23.

Benard, B. (1991). *Fostering resiliency in kids: Protective factors in the family, school, and community*. Portland, OR: Western Regional Center for Drug-Free Schools and Communities, Northwest Educational Laboratory.

Benard, B. (1999). Mentoring: New study shows the power of relationship to make a difference. In N. Henderson, B. Benard, N. Sharp-Light (Eds.), *Resiliency in action: Practical ideas for overcoming risks and building strengths in youth, families, & communities* (pp.93-99). Rio Rancho, NM: Resiliency In Action, Inc.

Benard, B. (1999). Focusing therapy on "what families do right": An interview with Steven Wolin, M.D. In N. Henderson, B. Benard, N. Sharp-Light (Eds.), *Resiliency in action: Practical ideas for overcoming risks and building strengths in youth, families, & communities* (pp.145-150). Rio Rancho, NM: Resiliency In Action,Inc.

Higgins, G.O. (1994). *Resilient adults: Overcoming a cruel past*. San Francisco: Jossey-Bass.

Resnick, et al. (1997). Protecting adolescents from harm: Findings from the National Longitudinal Study on Adolescent Health. *Journal of the American Medical Association 278* (10), 823-832.

Trout, S. (1999, January/February). A strength approach to adolescent development: A guide for parents and other caring adults. *Resiliency In Action*, 4-7.

USA Today. (October 8, 1998). Why are adults rude? Why so much pressure? (p. 8D).

Werner, E., & Smith, R. (1992). *Overcoming the odds: High risk children from birth to adulthood*. Ithaca, NY: Cornell University Press.

Werner, E. (1993, November). Presentation delivered at University of New Mexico School of Medicine conference, Albuquerque, NM.

Wolin, S., & Wolin, S. (1994). *Survivor's pride: Building resilience in youth at risk* (video). Verona, WI: Attainment Company.

Nan Henderson, M.S.W., is a national speaker and consultant on fostering resiliency and wellness, alcohol and other drug issues, and on organizational change. She has coauthored/edited five books about resiliency, and is the Editor-in-chief at Resiliency In Action, Inc. She can be reached at Nan Henderson and Associates, 5130 La Jolla Blvd., #2K, San Diego, CA 92109, p/f (858-488-5034), or by e-mail: (nanh@connectnet.com).

About the Editors of this Book

Nan Henderson, M.S.W., Bonnie Benard, M.S.W., and Nancy Sharp-Light share a strong commitment to shifting the national emphasis on "risk" to a recognition of the reality of resiliency. In 1996, drawing upon their combined backgrounds in social work, education, journalism, and business, they cofounded Resiliency In Action, Inc. The philosophy of the company, articulated by the three founders, is "resiliency is an innate self-righting and transcending ability within all children, youth, adults, organizations, and communities." The company mission is "to foster resiliency by disseminating resiliency-related information, facilitating the practical application and evaluation of the resiliency paradigm, and sustaining a national and international grass roots resiliency network."

Nan Henderson has been a clinical and school social worker; a statewide, citywide, and districtwide prevention program director; and a faculty member at several colleges and universities. She lives in San Diego, California, and now works as a consultant and speaker on fostering resiliency and wellness, and on school and organizational change. She is the coauthor of *Resiliency In Schools: Making it Happen for Students and Educators*, published in 1996 by Corwin Press; co-editor of *Resiliency In Action: Practical Ideas for Overcoming Risks and Building Strengths in Youth, Families, and Communities*, published in 1999 by Resiliency In Action, Inc.; and frequently contributes to national publications on the topic of resiliency. In 1997 she developed *The Resiliency Training Program*™, a training of trainers that has been used to train several hundred individuals from across the U.S. and other parts of the world.

Bonnie Benard has worked in the field of youth prevention for more than 20 years. She is widely recognized as a pioneer in the practical dissemination of social science research relevant to the well-being of children and youth, and currently lives in Berkeley, California. She has authored numerous publications on the prevention of youth risk behaviors and on fostering resiliency, including *Fostering Resiliency in Kids: Protective Factors in Family, School, and Community* and *Turning the Corner from Risk to Resiliency*. She is also co-editor of *Resiliency In Action: Practical Ideas for Overcoming Risks and Building Strengths in Youth, Families, and Communities*, published in 1999 by Resiliency In Action, Inc.; a frequent contributor to national publications; and a speaker and consultant on fostering resiliency and wellness in children, youth, and families.

Nancy Sharp-Light has been in the field of education since 1972 as a teacher, prevention counselor, and director of substance abuse prevention programs. She lives in Rio Rancho, New Mexico, where she now works as an educational consultant, writer, and national trainer. She is co-editor of *Resiliency In Action: Practical Ideas for Overcoming Risks and Building Strengths in Youth, Families, and Communities*, published in 1999 by Resiliency In Action, Inc.; and has written numerous curriculum, including a community-based program for substance abusing adolescents and their families, which won several awards. Her resiliency-promoting parenting curriculum, *We're Doing the Best We Can*, is the result of her many years working with multi-cultural populations in New Mexico and across the country. In 1988, she was selected as the outstanding teacher in the state of New Mexico.

Speeches, Presentations, and Training
From The Editors at Resiliency In Action, Inc.

Nan Henderson, M.S.W.: *Nan Henderson and Associates, 5130 La Jolla Blvd., #2K, San Diego, CA 92109, t/f (858) 488-5034; nanh@connectnet.com*
- "How Families, Schools, and Communities Foster Resilient Children"
- "Resiliency in Schools and other Organizations: Making it Happen"
- "Four Steps to Resiliency"
- "*The Resiliency Training Program*™ Training of Trainers

Craig Noonan, Ph.D.c: *Alternatives, 5130 La Jolla Blvd., #2K, San Diego, CA 92109, t/f (858) 488-5034; wnoonan@popmail.ucsd.edu*
- "Integrating Resiliency and Effective Counseling Practice"
- "No Fault Counseling: How People Change Problematic Behavior"
- "Empowering and Effective Brief Intervention"
- "A Step-by-Step Guide to Program Evaluation"

Nancy Sharp-Light: *Sharp-Light Consulting, 602 San Juan de Rio, Rio Rancho, NM 87124 t/f(505) 891-1350; nslight@aol.com (or nslight@RTgraphics.com)*
- "Team-Building for Resilience"
- "Classroom Techniques for Moving Students from Stress to Success "
- "KidBitz: How to Present Anything to Anyone." For youth involved in any activities, such as Service-Learning Projects, requiring public contacts and presentations.

PRODUCT INFORMATION

RESILIENCY IN ACTION: Practical Ideas for Overcoming Risks and Building Strengths in Youth, Families, & Communities

Nan Henderson, Bonnie Benard, Nancy Sharp-Light, ed.
Foreword by Peter Benson, Ph.D., President of Search Institute
1999, 180 pages, 2nd Printing (Paperback)

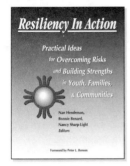

* *"Bursting with new ideas, exemplars of best practices...and interviews with individuals–leaders and pioneers in the field–who have been doing resiliency work for years. Ahead of the curve."*
    —**Dennis Saleeby, Ph.D.**, University of Kansas, Editor of *The Strengths Perspective in Social Work Practice*
* *"This is the bible for our work!"*
    —**Barbara Keller**, Executive Director, Suffolk Coalition to Prevent Alcohol and Drug Dependencies, Happauge, NY
* *"A resource that changes hearts and minds."*
    —**Brenda Holben**, Safe and Drug-Free Schools Coordinator, Cherry Creek Schools, CO

Single Copy
$28.95
ISBN 0-9669394-0-9

A one-of-a-kind resource to guide every aspect of fostering resiliency in children, youth, families, and communities. Contents include: The Foundations of Resiliency; Resiliency and Schools; Resiliency and Communities; Creating Connections: Mentoring, Support, and Peer Programs; Resiliency and Youth (including asset) Development; and Resiliency and Families. Each section is filled with easy-to-understand research reports and ways that the research is being applied. The "must have" book for schools, agencies, and community organizations as they meet the challenges of the next decade.

SCHOOLWIDE APPROACHES FOR FOSTERING RESILIENCY

Nan Henderson, Bonnie Benard, Nancy Sharp-Light, ed.
Introduction by Barbara Wotherspoon, School Principal, Newton, NH
1999, 109 pages (Paperback)

How do schools currently build resiliency in students and staff, and how can they do the job better? Based on the research-proven assumption that "effective education" and "fostering resiliency" go hand-in-hand, this book offers

* practical steps all schools can take to foster resiliency in students and staff
* an understanding of how building resiliency is the foundation of effective education, and vice versa
* resiliency-building perspectives from principals
* teaching strategies that are proven resiliency builders
* ways to assess and improve schoolwide resiliency building
* suggestions for creating safe, violence-free schools
* an annotated bibliography

Single Copy
$12.95
ISBN 0-9669394-2-5

Originally published as articles in the journal *Resiliency In Action*, this book also contains new, never-before published information.

PRODUCT INFORMATION

Mentoring for Resiliency: *Setting Up Programs for Moving Youth from "Stressed to Success"*

Nan Henderson, Bonnie Benard, Nancy Sharp-Light, ed.
Introduction by Emmy Werner, Ph.D., University of California
1999, 90 pages, (Paperback)

What are the crucial elements of all successful mentoring programs? This book has the answers from

- Marc Freedman, M.A., considered the "guru" of the mentoring movement;
- Bonnie Benard, M.S.W., the most widely read author on resiliency in the U.S.;
- Emmy Werner, Ph.D., known as the "mother" of resiliency research;
- Ralph Renger, Ph.D., and his colleagues, who offer a "guidebook" for mentoring program design; and
- Nan Henderson, M.S.W., who has interviewed many resilient youth–including those who have bounced back from risk behavior due to the relationships they had with mentors.
    Originally published as articles in the journal *Resiliency In Action*, this book also contains new, never-before published information.

Single Copy
$12.95
ISBN 0-9669394-1-7

Four Steps to Resiliency... the pamphlet you've been waiting for!

$25.00 per package of 50

Nan Henderson, M.S.W
Pamphlets in packages of 50

This is the pamphlet our readers have been asking for! In down-to-earth language, resiliency is defined, and four important steps anyone can take to foster resiliency in themselves and others are presented. Illustrated. Includes resources for further reading. Order for parents, educators, law makers, community groups, and youth.

Back issues of the journal *Resiliency In Action*

This quarterly journal is now discontinued but all back issues are available—some may be photocopied.
$7.00 each (original and photocopied)

- Premier Issue: Foundations of Resiliency
- Resiliency and Schools
- Resiliency and Communities
- Creating Connections for Resiliency: Mentoring, Support, and Peer Programs
- Resiliency and Youth Development
- Resiliency and Families
- Resiliency and the Mind-Body Connection
- Resiliency and Gender

- Changing the "At Risk" Paradigm
- Resiliency and the Arts
- Resiliency and Gender
- Resiliency and Politics
- Werner Research Update/Service Learning
- "It Takes a Child to Raise a Whole Village"/ Resiliency in Prisons
- Resiliency and Self-Esteem/Adolescence from a Strength Perspective

TO ORDER SEE PAGE 87

ORDER FORM

MAIL WITH YOUR **PO** TO:
> RESILIENCY IN ACTION
> BOX 45240
> RIO RANCHO, NM 87174-5240
OR **FAX** WITH YOUR **PO** TO:
> (505) 891-1350
OR **CALL TOLL FREE:**
> (800) 440-5171
OR ORDER **ON-LINE** AT:
> WWW.RESILIENCY.COM

Quantity Discounts		
1-10	Copies:	Price as listed
11-25	Copies of the same title:	10% discount
26-50	Copies of the same title:	20% discount
51+	Copies of the same title	25% discount

FED. ID #85-0438768

(**PLEASE PRINT!**)

Qty.	Unit Price	Description	Price

PLEASE REMEMBER TO ADD 15%

SHIPPING AND HANDLING

TO EACH ORDER

TOTAL ORDER	
15% S/H	
SUBTOTAL	
NM RESIDENTS ADD TAX 6.1875%	
TOTAL AMOUNT DUE	

PLEASE SHIP TO :   (**PLEASE PRINT!**)

NAME _____

ORGANIZATION _____

ADDRESS _____

CITY _____ STATE _____ ZIP _____

PHONE (   )_____ FAX (   )_____

E-MAIL _____ PROFESSION _____

BILL TO (IF DIFFERENT) : (PLEASE ATTACH **PO** TO THIS FORM)

ORGANIZATION_____

ATTN. _____

ADDRESS _____

CITY _____ STATE _____ ZIP _____

PHONE (   )_____ FAX (   )_____

E-MAIL _____

METHOD OF PAYMENT :

☐ CHECK ENCLOSED (CK # _____)

☐ PURCHASE ORDER ATTACHED: PO# _____

☐ CREDIT CARD

MC ☐ (MasterCard)   V ☐ VISA   AMX ☐ ▨

CC#_____ EXP. DATE _____

CARD HOLDER'S SIGNATURE _____